The Encounter with God

ASPECTS OF MODERN THEOLOGY

The Encounter with God

>>>>><<<<<

ASPECTS OF MODERN THEOLOGY

Edited by
Joseph E. O'Neill, S.J.

with a Foreword by
John Courtney Murray, S.J.

THE MACMILLAN COMPANY >> NEW YORK
MACMILLAN NEW YORK, LONDON

The Macmillan Company, New York
Collier-Macmillan Canada, Ltd., Galt, Ontario
Divisions of The Crowell-Collier Publishing Company

First Printing

NIHIL OBSTAT
    EDWARD J. MONTANO, S.T.D.
    CENSOR LIBRORUM

IMPRIMATUR
    ✠ FRANCIS CARDINAL SPELLMAN
    ARCHBISHOP OF NEW YORK

IMPRIMI POTEST:
    JOHN J. MCGINTY, S.J.
    PRAEP. PROV. NEO EBORACENSIS

The nihil obstat and imprimatur are
official declarations that a book or pam-
phlet is free of doctrinal or moral error.
No implication is contained therein that
those who have granted the nihil obstat
and imprimatur agree with the contents,
opinions or statements expressed.

Printed in the United States of America

Library of Congress catalog card number: 62-19426

CONTENTS

Foreword   vii
             John Courtney Murray, S.J.

Introduction   xi
             Joseph E. O'Neill, S.J.

Miracles and Contemporary Theology   1
             Robert W. Gleason, S.J.

Some Aspects of Current Christology   33
             Thomas E. Clarke, S.J.

Mary Is the Church   59
             Quentin Quesnell, S.J.

The Sacraments in Theology Today   80
             Matthew J. O'Connell, S.J.

Symbolism and Kerygmatic Theology   107
             Herbert Musurillo, S.J.

The Preacher and the Historical Witness of the
   Gospels   138
             Francis J. McCool, S.J.

The Encounter with God   177
             P. De Letter, S.J.

FOREWORD

THE editor of a periodical is inclined to avoid visiting the periodical room in libraries. The experience is too depressing. Shelf upon shelf of magazines, filled with material that was laboriously solicited, edited, proofread, published, bound—and buried. The inquiring scholar will now and again dig out the articles of higher quality; but he must dig. Therefore the editor of the present volume has prolonged his usefulness and enhanced the merit of his original service by rescuing from possible, and quite undeserved, oblivion the articles here republished. Their authors will be gratified.

What is more important, a wider public will be assisted in the fulfillment of a duty that today has become pressing. I mean the duty of developing a theological culture in America. It is not too much to speak of a duty. It is imposed, first of all, from within, in virtue of the possession of the Christian faith. The seat of faith is the intelligence of man, even though the light of the truth descends, as it were, into the intelligence through the will that loves the light and purposes to follow whither it leads. The assent of faith settles, by firm answer, the final question that all men must face, "What, in the end, is the meaning of life and its value?" The answer is in the data of revelation, as formulated in the dogmas of the Church. These affirmations of faith are final, as affirmations; their truth is not subject to question by the Christian. Nonetheless, history is witness to the fact that the affirmations of faith, at the same time that they settle the issue of truth, also raise a manifold issue of understanding. And the Christian who would fulfill the exigencies of his own faith must face this issue too.

The data of revelation, in the Scripture, are scattered; the dogmas of the Church, which have been defined within historical circumstances of error, are fragments of a larger truth. Both the dogma and the revealed data bear upon the great enveloping mystery called the order of grace, which is the mystery of God and of his redemptive love for us, manifested by the Word Incarnate and by the outpouring of His Holy Spirit. Faith is the adherence to this mystery. But the adherence itself gives rise to the constant duty of Christians to penetrate more deeply into the data of revelation, to think out in freshly illuminating forms the organic unity of the full revelation, in order to arrive at a more profound understanding of the Christian mystery, in itself, in its intimate relevance to the whole of human life, and in its meaning for all the enterprises in which man is engaged in this world. This is what is meant by theology. It is a work of reason enlightened by faith, or, more exactly, of faith making use of reason to reach an understanding of itself. The result is the progressive formation of the true Christian mind, in which faith has had its proper flowering in a theological culture. Within the Church this culture is an indispensable necessity.

Never more so than today, when the crisis of culture in our postmodern age has become acute. A simple faith, so called, that is, a faith that has been accepted without being assimilated by the mind, is per se sufficient for the salvation of one's soul. Whether it is likewise sufficient in the circumstances of today may well be questioned. In any case, it is not sufficient for the fulfillment of the mission of the Church in the temporal order, as this mission confronts the Christian community—especially the lay Christian community—in this historical moment. The earthly vocation of the Church, as a force for human culture and civilization, is indeed secondary and subordinate, an overflow of the pursuance of its essential mission, which is to establish a kingdom that is not of this world. Nonetheless, a divine imperative lies behind this earthly vocation. A Christianity divorced from the realities of this world, and without impact on the course of history, would be untrue to itself. "The greatest fault of Christians in the twentieth century," said Cardinal Suhard, "would be to leave the world to shape itself and to bring itself to unity without them." But effective participation in this task of shaping the world, bringing it to unity, fulfilling its aspirations for freedom and for greater justice, supposes the possession of a theological culture, wedded to faith, and widespread among the people of God.

The fact should be evident. And it makes evident the value of this book. All of its essays have the double merit of being theological in the high sense and also pertinent to problems of the moment. The thought that they contain, and the mode of thinking that they illustrate, will make (so one greatly hopes) for the desired development of a theological culture among us.

John Courtney Murray, S.J.

INTRODUCTION

EDUCATED Catholics today, more than ever before, are interested in their religion and in the theology of their religion. This is not only out of solicitude for the growth of the spirit, nor only out of need to solve the perplexities and to relieve the tensions of the nuclear age; it is also out of a desire to drink more deeply of the wellsprings of Revelation as it is revealed through Scripture and Tradition. In particular, they are eager to learn more of the speculative thinking that has been done and is being done concerning the great truths of theology.

Further, educated Catholics are more fully aware than ever before that ignorance is not a blessing but an obstacle to the successful pursuit of truth and virtue alike and therefore to that triumph of the spirit which is of the intellect and the will. Catholic men and women today, even as the men and women of other faiths, are truly stirred with the new excitement sweeping through the ancient halls of theology, the fresh breeze that is creating new movements, new trends and approaches. And they are more and more coming to the realization that theology is not a mass of static facts, a collection of fossilized relics of what was once alive and breathing but a vital, living thing because truth is living and because truth is a Person. Therefore they are interested in theology as the living truth about that Divine Person and all else in relation to Him.

The pages that follow are an attempt by a group of Jesuit theologians to keep abreast of certain especially important aspects of modern theology. All these essays appeared originally in *Thought*, with the exception of "The Preacher and the Historical Witness of the Gospels." The Reverend John Courtney Murray, S.J., the noted theologian and editor of *Theological Studies*, graciously gave permission for its inclusion and himself has contributed a stimulating foreword to the work.

The first aspect to be discussed is very properly that of the concept of miracles. The Reverend Robert W. Gleason, S.J., offers an illuminating treatment of the nature of miracles as seen in the light of contemporary theology. The importance of the theme is obvious: the recognition and the acceptance of miracles are a step in the direction of Christ and of His Church.

But what are theologians saying of Christ today? This is the natural question to be asked next and it is fully answered by the Reverend Thomas E. Clarke, S.J., who concludes from an examination of the evidence at hand that the principal trends in current Christology are toward integration, balance and transition.

No significant approach to Christ, the God-man, could be complete without the further step to Mary and to the Church, and no theology could be impervious to the natural and supernatural relationship between the two. That the relationship is of the closest nature is the strongly argued contention of the Reverend Quentin Quesnell, S.J., who maintains that Mary is the Church and the Church is Mary and this because they are both the supreme participators of the redemption form, the salvation pattern, which is Christ.

From Christ have come the sacraments. Signs and symbols, they are also ecclesial actions whose symbolism is of paramount interest to modern theologians. As a result of his careful survey, the Reverend Matthew O'Connell, S.J., concludes that sacramental theology today is beginning to see these actions once again as they appeared to St. Augustine and his Greek peers, heavy with the age-old desires of religious man, and adopted by the creative will of Christ to be symbols of the living faith and hope of His mystical body.

Next, the Reverend Herbert Musurillo, S.J., discusses with insight the problem of symbolic communication at the heart of all Christian literature and the complexity and importance which it has for the life of the Christian today, especially for that of the theologian whose role it is to express and develop in humanly intelligible symbols the primitive message of Christian Revelation in the concrete context of time and space.

For the preacher, however, the proclamation of the word of Christ as revealed in Scripture is the primary duty. But how can he know for certain that he has truly grasped the truth of Scripture? How can he be certain of his own interpretation of Scripture? How, in short, is the preacher to move with assurance through the maze of new developments in the area of Scriptural exegesis? Concentrating on one concern of the preacher, his preoccupation with the modern exegete's admission that the Gospels are not "pure" historical sources, and confining himself to a single parable of the Gospel, the Reverend Francis J. McCool, S.J., describes in fascinating detail the process by which the trained historian and biblical scholar goes about the difficult and delicate task of reconstructing the life and work of Christ on the basis of the Gospel tradition.

Finally, there is the problem, so interesting to modern theologians, of the nature of the encounter with God. What precisely happens ontologically and psychologically in the meeting between the individual human person and the God of all truth? This is the problem raised and this is the question answered by the Reverend P. De Letter, S.J. In the course of his significant discussion he throws new light upon the mystery of grace and the hidden riches to be found in the personalistic approach to Christ and the Triune God.

These seven essays then are a modest attempt to answer a modern need and a modern desire in a modern way. But in addition to the need and the desire there is also a modern obligation. Father Murray has stated it succintly as "the duty of developing a theological culture in America." It is the common hope of the makers of this little book that their efforts will have resulted in some small contribution to so worthy a cause.

Joseph E. O'Neill, S.J.

Robert W. Gleason

>>>>><<<<<

MIRACLES AND
CONTEMPORARY THEOLOGY

In THEOLOGICAL writings about miracles today
there is somewhat less uniformity of opinion than obtained
in the eighteenth and most of the nineteenth century. The
definition of miracle, its relation to natural laws and its
knowability have been widely discussed. Since miracles are
so intimately bound up with the Christian faith, it is perhaps
worthwhile to outline somewhat briefly the controverted
positions and to see their development in the Scriptures and
tradition.

Sacred Scripture presents us with the description of

1

prodigies that manifest God's goodness and power and point to the existence of a world beyond the visible. The Old Testament has as one of its central themes the marvelous deeds worked by God for His chosen people and His command over nature and history. Jahweh is great and incomprehensible; His deeds are causes for wonderment. They are strange, manifesting the presence of a holy and terrible God whose sovereignty extends over all creation.[1]

The Old Testament understands the miracle not only as a physical prodigy but as a sign given to confirm the faith of a people who constantly demonstrated their need for confirmation. Hence Jahweh's miracles are most conspicuous at the time of the Exodus and again at those periods when His power had to be clearly upheld in opposition to that of the Baals of Israel's neighbors. Creation itself is ordered to the covenant and all reality proclaims the greatness of God whose power is unlimited. Nothing is impossible to Him; He can give victory as He chooses. The history of Israel is itself viewed as a prodigious ordering of secular history by God to Israel's salvation. History is not simply an orderly succession of events but a divine, continuous creation.

The physical prodigy is a concrete and concentrated manifestation of God's powerful protection of Israel. Having always the function of a sign, it leads men to acknowledge the transcendent hidden God whose wonderful deeds arouse awe and faith.

Moses is granted the power to produce miracles, as an instrument of God, because he has the task of confirming the faith of His people. Isaias is aware that he can produce whatever sign Achaz may ask, for the faith of the king is at stake. But the great miracle of the Old Testament remains Israel herself, experiencing continually in her history the active intervention of God.[2] The crossing of the Red Sea is the prototype of God's wonderful actions in Israel's behalf: Moses is present to fit this event into a religious context and to interpret its value as a sign of God's faithful intentions.

For the Israelite the concept of miracle is never divorced from that of sign: a miracle takes place at a particular time, in a particular arrangement of circumstances which sets in evidence God's marvelous intervention in behalf of His covenanted people. "Here, then," said the Lord, "is the covenant I will make. Before the eyes of all your people I will work such marvels as have never been wrought in any nation anywhere on earth, so that this people among whom you live may see how awe-inspiring are the deeds which I, the Lord, will do at your side" (Ex. 34,10). According to the Old Testament the deepest meaning of the miracle lies in this connection of the prodigy performed and the invitation to faith that it contains. Hence at the beginning of the prophetic age when faith in God had to be sustained against the encroachment of syncretism, miracles will be frequent. During the exile they will also be needed to reassure a defeated people as they encounter a powerful civilization and its false gods. Each period of crisis calls for a new demonstration of Jahweh's power and invites anew to faith.[3]

The interpreter of the miracle is normally present in the person of a prophet who judges history and events and reads the sign to the people. The people have the role of witnesses to God's superiority over the gods of the nations and the miracle is given to testify to this superiority. Israel is to see that in contrast to Egypt's limited powers, Jahweh is supremely powerful. The Israelites are to realize that the dominion of Jahweh extends also over the Assyrians. He can use foreigners to chastise Israel because they too fall under His marvelous dominion. Jahweh alone is the controlling force of history, its directing will. His free choice of Israel over other nations indicates that His power is universal. He can lead the Philistines where He will; he can use Assyria as a rod because history and creation are utterly subject to Him who is subject to no one. Nothing is too wonderful for His power. "The Lord said to Abraham, "Why did Sara laugh, saying, 'Shall I indeed bear a child, although I am old?' Is anything too wonderful for the Lord?" (Gen. 18,13-14).

The wonderful deeds of Jahweh invite to faith; they also point to the future, to the last times, when the final kingdom of God will be established. The new earth and new heavens of Isaias are foretold by the miracle with its demonstration of the submission of earthly reality to the will of Jahweh. When He comes to dwell among His people His coming will have been announced ahead of time by His prodigious deeds for the people of the covenant. Israel's miraculous history will then find its fulfillment.

The classic type of miracle—the crossing of the Red Sea —demonstrates the pattern of the Old Testament miracle. The miracle consists in this, that at a particular time and with a particular meaning a crossing was made possible by Jahweh as a sign of His presence in Israel's midst. The elements involved are a physical prodigy, the presence of an interpreter, and a meaning attached, pointing to the future of Israel. To Israel this passing of the Red Sea was no unaccountable freak of nature, but the response of nature to the summons of nature's maker.[4] Miriam's song celebrated it with the words: "Sing to the Lord for he is gloriously triumphant: horse and chariot he has cast into the sea." (Ex. 15,21).

Israel's concept of a miracle was not precisely that of "an exception to a natural law." When Israel reflected upon a universe governed by stable laws she wondered at their constancy and stability, taking them as occasions to glorify Jahweh who so established the world in harmony. But she did not possess the idea of a self-sustaining universe, an independent realm of laws from which God is absent. He sustains His creation and it submits to His will. Simple natural events and great prodigies as well are all expressions of this will. God is constantly active in history, molding history and events and the universe for the purposes He has in mind for His covenanted people. The regular turn of the seasons, the fall of rain, the growth of crops express God's will. He is not withdrawn from his creation; at moments of crisis, He makes His presence felt in a special manner in His wonderful deeds. After all, His very name is wonderful. It is to be expected that "signs" and "wonders" should fall from His guiding hand. An extraordinary event, or an extraordinary concursus of events, assumes the importance of a sign, because to the Israelite God is not aloof from the world but immediately present. To Him, in the ultimate analysis, must be ascribed both the regular course of human life and its extraordinary moments. When His presence is pointed out in a special way, when a national prodigy summons the people again to a belief in His active presence in their midst, they would speak of a miracle. It was an event of profound significance because it spoke to them of God's activity in their favor. The Israelites did not attempt a rational, philosophic analysis of nature and her limits. The entire world is a miracle of God and the idea of miracle is implied in God's creative activity. Nature, which in awe-inspiring phenomenon reveals God's presence, is viewed as the immediate and mysterious work of God. To Israel nature has not the hostile and terrifying aspects it could assume in other religions because it is totally submissive to Him.[5]

God's work in history is accompanied by revelation and this concept of the close connection between miracle and prophetic revelation dates from the beginning of Israel's religious convictions. Belief in God is firmly based upon the fact of His activity in history and history is the background against which Israel's faith stands out. Having intervened in behalf of this oppressed people, He called her into being as a people, a fact to which the prophets constantly point. By His activity for the salvation of His people He reveals Himself as the living and present God, faithful, holy and just. Israel's destiny is controlled by God who intervenes to judge and to save: His interventions are awe-inspiring and majestic but they lead to faith and love. The great event, fixed forever in Israel's national consciousness, was the crossing of the Red Sea.[6]

It would be quite futile to interrogate the Old Testament concerning a "scientific" concept of miracle. The whole burden of Israel's faith is that Jahweh is the transcendent Lord of nature which He submits to His saving will. The people survived every crisis on the basis of this faith. To examine the natural laws which provided the framework for God's rescue did not interest the Hebrew. The fact was clear: over and over again God bent natural forces to His desire to save a helpless people. To seek to explain the wonder of the Exodus on purely natural grounds would have seemed futile and absurd to the Hebrew. Jahweh can and did work wonders in delivering His people. The Hebrew did not debate whether these were done by an exception to natural laws or not. Nature and the constant operations of nature are subject to a personality outside of nature: Jahweh. The operations of nature are themselves a wonder: Jahweh's control of nature and history for Israel's salvation is a wonder. At the heart of the Exodus story is the historical fact that God intervened in a marvelous fashion to shape history and submit nature to His plans. Israel's faith was based upon actual events in which it perceived the hand of God.

In sum we might say of Israel that her faith was based upon miracles: that miracles, while not scientifically examined, were understood as Jahweh's direct and wonderful interventions in history and nature to stand as signs inviting to faith and pointing to the last days when His kingdom would be fulfilled.

As the Old Testament had seen miracles to be a proof of God's intervention in favor of His people, so the New Testament presented Christ's miracles as a proof of His divine mission. In His public life Christ Himself had pointed to His works as confirmation of His divine mission.[7] Throughout the first centuries following His death the Church again referred to Christ's miracles to establish the rational grounds for belief, His deeds being sufficient indication of His divinity. But there was as yet little scientific speculation concerning the precise nature of a miracle or its relation to faith. The word "miracle," as late as the fourth century, had many varied meanings in Christian writings. For Augustine a miracle may mean an extraordinary and marvelous event which is the product of angelic or diabolic power, the prodigies performed by pagan gods, or that which is prodigious, unexpected and contrary to what we know of the course of nature. Later, Augustinians were to interpret Augustine as having understood by a miracle that which transcends the operation of natural causes and requires the intervention of God. Augustine also believed that God, the author of nature, had implanted certain virtualities in creatures which could respond to His activity and thus allow them to produce the miraculous occurence when God so willed.[8]

Further speculation on the nature of a miraculous event was indulged in by the successors of Augustine who stressed the revealing character of a prodigy, that is, as indicating the presence of the divine power, and pointing to an order above nature and produced outside of or contrary to the customary order of natural causes. St. Thomas made the next and decisive step when he defined a miracle as that which is contrary to the usual course of nature. Hence the element of the startling, the unexpected, the prodigious is played down since, as St. Thomas remarks, "even though a thing took place everyday, it would be a miracle if it were beyond the order of all created nature" (*S.T.*I., q. 110, a. 4). In addition, St. Thomas recognizes as a strict miracle only that which the angels or devils could not do of their own power but which requires the action of God.[9]

Benedict XIV in his classic work *De servorum Dei beatificatione et beatorum canonizatione* modifies St. Thomas' position somewhat in conceding that an effect produced by angelic forces, acting by their own power, with divine approbation, may be called a miracle. It would, however, be called only a minor miracle, the term "major" being reserved for those miracles which surpass the forces of *all* created nature, including the angelic, and demand God for their author. Benedict also stressed that in evaluating the phenomena we must look to the religious *purpose* of the event. A true miracle has a clearly religious purpose and is directed to the confirmation of truth or of personal sanctity. This line of thinking was further developed by many Catholic theologians of the nineteenth century. Confronted with phenomena in the religions of pagan Greece, India, China and Rome which bore some external resemblance to the wonders of the Old and the New Testament, these theologians distinguished the true miracle as one produced by God and His benevolent angels, while admitting that God might permit diabolic agencies to bring about externally similar phenomena through their native powers. The character of the event, the *purpose*, the *method*, the *circumstances* and the *moral effects* will indicate whether the agent is Divine, angelic, or diabolical.[10] Not all theologians agreed with this position, some preferring to restrict the term "miracle" to those events which transcend the powers of all created natures including those of the angels and devils. However, by the beginning of the twentieth century the distinction between major and minor miracles had gained ground and today is more commonly admitted. The fact that an event surpasses the visible and corporeal forces of nature is sufficient to establish it as a miracle, if its character manifests that its author is either God or an angel. The event transcends human forces and this marks it as miraculous, granted that the purpose, method, circumstances and moral effects all point to God or an angel as its author.[11]

Catholic theologians in the twentieth century have often stressed the *sign aspect* of a miracle, something which had been somewhat less emphasized as long as the aspect of transcendence was being debated. They are by no means, however, unanimously in agreement as to the definition of a miracle, but there is evident a general tendency to insist upon its religious context and its value as a divine sign. Many insist also upon the fact that a miracle is a fact perceptible by the senses. Some Thomists, such as Garrigou-Lagrange, adhere very closely to the position of St. Thomas, refusing even to extend the term "miracle" in a strict sense to cover prodigious events accomplished by angelic forces with the approbation of God. They prefer to denominate such events as relative miracles, miracles *secundum quid*, that is, events verifying the definition of miracle only analogously. Others who also insist that a miracle must be perceptible by the senses do not consider suprasensible events such as the virginal conception of Christ as miracles, perferring to call them "miraculous facts." Marcozzi suggests that their principal preoccupation is to tailor the definition of miracles to the statement of the Vatican Council (Denzinger, 1790) that miracles are "most certain signs" of divine revelation.

Those theologians who stress the note of sign in miracles are clearly turning back to Augustine for whom the preternatural aspect of miracles was less important than that of sign. For Augustine all events were signs of God's power and His love for humanity; the change of water into wine at Cana is astounding, but the appearance of wine-grapes each year is also marvelous. God works miracles to astonish us when we become too accustomed to the daily exercise of His forces in nature and need more striking signs. In the face of ordinary routine life we tend to become blinded to God's presence, so He arouses us by a prodigious sign of His divine power and goodness. Miracles are not just prodigies, they are religious prodigies in a definite context and are a communication from God to man. Christ's healings in the Gospel stress the goodness and mercy of God; they manifest His omnipotence and bounty, and the context in which they take place invites us to faith and gratitude. They are the specific signs of a whole new order established in the world by Christ Jesus who has been sent for the redemption of the world.[12] Outside of this religious context the physical prodigy would be unintelligible. E. Dhanis remarks that the extraordinary event assumes in its context the character of a reply or a sign from God; it is a testimony of God's good will, of warning, of teaching, a seal of approval on doctrines and persons. The extraordinary event in question is so closely linked to a particular religious context that we are able to perceive it as a divine intervention.[13]

Other authors stress the notion of context and sign to such an extent as to find quite incomplete the definition of miracle as an event that surpasses the laws of nature. In their eyes certain Scholastic authors have viewed miracles too exclusively from the viewpoint of efficient cause and not sufficiently from the aspect of final causes.[14] As a result it often seemed that one had only to consider the preternatural aspect of the event to decide whether or not it was miraculous. With some authors today the pendulum has swung completely in the opposite direction. For them the transcendence of a miracle is not disclosed to us in the fact that it surpasses the capacities of nature, but the religious context makes evident that this extraordinary, baffling, beneficial event, a sign of God's message to us, is not produced by natural agencies. Seen in its total context it is clear that the author of the event can only be God, and not a natural agency. Hence the miracle has a double element, an observable fact and the religious meaning *inherent* in this fact. The physical event in all its extraordinariness is a necessary part of the miracle, but it remains secondary in its importance, its full significance comprehensible only in the light of its context, its doctrinal signification, its role as part of a dialogue between God and men.[15]

Consequently some think that the surpassing of nature's capacities should not be stressed as the essential element in a miracle; they point out that to define a miracle in this way is of little practical value since one can never establish with certainty that a given fact is a violation of nature.

Guy de Broglie has commented at length on these two conceptions and on the apologetic value of miracles. His major objection to too great a divorce between the physical event and the doctrine it confirms is that in the concrete it is very difficult to prove scientifically that an event is attributable to God alone, if one divorces it from the context of the doctrine it confirms.[16] And he remarks that it is more difficult than appears at first sight to establish that a certain physical operation is exclusively proper to God. Creation *ex nihilo* is certainly an instance, but the cases are perhaps limited where one can prove by strictly metaphysical arguments that only God could have produced this effect. Could we domonstrate metaphysically that only God can calm a tempest, change water into wine, give sight to the blind? An apologetic of miracles which claims to establish scientifically the divine origin of prodigies from considerations of a purely physical and metaphysical nature inevitably ends up enmeshed in inextricable difficulties. It is quite difficult to prove scientifically the concrete realization of those rare actions whose very nature permits us to reserve them to God alone. How can we establish with scientific exactitude that in the case of a particular raising of a dead man the soul actually had left the body? De Broglie believes that the more sane approach to an apologetic of miracles is to place the physical event fully in its religious context. Christian miracles are complementary signs and cannot be separated from the other fundamental signs that testify to the Christian message, that is, *the excellence of the doctrine* of Christ and the divine *transcendence* of the virtues he displayed. They must be considered in their concrete liaison with the doctrine of the Gospels themselves. The divine transcendence of Christ's doctrine pleads effectively for the truth of the doctrine and the concrete manifestation of divine life pleads effectively for the divine authority of Christ and the Church. Miracles are complementary signs, subsidiary and accidental, linked to the more fundamental signs. They have their full normal value only in conjunction with doctrine and sanctity.[17]

Maurice Blondel had long ago objected to what he considered an unnatural separation of the physical event of a miracle from its context and doctrinal meaning.[18] His viewpoint was that a miracle was not strictly speaking an exception to the laws of nature since nature does not have such fixed laws. In a miracle we have an extraordinary event, unexplainable, baffling, unparalleled, in sharp contrast to the ordinary course of events—a physical *prodigy*. This prodigy is intrinsically linked with doctrine so that the doctrine illuminates the event and the event confirms the doctrine. Possibly the brute fact is explainable by natural laws, but in the situation God provides adequate proof of His intervention.

It is useless to attempt a proof, *more geometrico*, of a miracle by applying deductive philosophical principles or experimental methods. One must interpret the event by its religious significance which is as form to the matter of the prodigy. This is an event for the benefit of mankind, which points to the supernatural world, completely woven into a doctrinal and religious context and unexplainable and unintelligible without that context. Because it can be grasped only as what it is, in a particular religious context, it definitely bears the stamp of divine intervention, bearing a message to man from God. The circumstances in which it occurs are the ultimate reason that it can be seen as "transcending" the law of nature. But the attempt first to discover the laws of nature and all their possibilities is useless.

Without endorsing Blondel's position and in fact while rejecting his particular understanding of the transcendence of nature, recent writers have tried to bring to the fore again those elements in tradition which Blondel had emphasized. François Taymans notes that when the Vatican Council declared that miracles are most certain signs of revelation which manifest God's power and goodness, it harmonized two aspects of tradition: the fact that a miraculous event has an exceptional character, which the ordinary and normal course of nature does not explain, and the fact that it occurs in a religious context.[19] If Anselm neglected the sign aspect of miracle, St. Thomas did not (S.T. III, q. 43, a. 4). But the emphasis of St. Thomas' writings, as with those scholastics who followed him, was primarily fixed upon the efficient cause. Non-Catholic authors often deduced from popular theology manuals that the Church decided whether or not an event was a miracle by an appeal to its transcendence of natural causes, without any consideration of its context. Moreover, the objections raised against the possibility of miracles often reveal the inadequacy of the concept, as though the fact, isolated from its context were intelligible in itself. Taymans insists that a miracle is a sign and that one cannot understand it separated from the reality it signifies. As a sign of Revelation it is a sign of a specific new order, the supernatural order. Precisely because it is a sign of an order superior to nature, it must in itself be recognizable as superior to the order of natural causality. A miracle is therefore a sensible sign which the habitual course of nature does not explain but which God produces in a religious context as a sign of the supernatural.

It is interesting to note that Taymans does not insist upon the note "constituting an exception to natural laws." A miracle certainly contradicts the common and stable observations of mankind, but not necessarily natural laws understood as principles founded critically and scientifically. Were it a miracle only if it did so, the miracle would lose its value as sign for the ordinary man; and the witnesses of the miracles of the Old and New Testaments were not ordinarily scientists. A scientist can have certitude concerning a miracle, but so can a prudent yet unscientific intelligence. This certitude is certainly prescientific, but it is none the less real and sufficient to justify prudent assent. Taymans notes also that Christian tradition has included in the number of Christ's miracles a number of events which the ordinary course of nature does not easily explain and yet which *could* be produced by natural causes. In the concrete religious context in which they were produced, one becomes aware that, although nature might be their author, absolutely speaking, in the context, God is the author. That Christ should order the apostles to let down their nets at a particular spot and time after a fruitless night to catch a great draft of fishes makes it evident that He has intervened. The concept of "exception to the laws of nature" must be sufficiently fluid to allow for such events.

Part of the context of a miracle is precisely the appeal made to God; men pray, wait, hope, and God responds.

In a particularly judicious article on the subject, E. Dhanis notes that certain Catholic philosophers and theologians today have a tendency to abstract from the idea of an "exception to natural laws."[20] He is careful to explain that this formula "exception to natural laws" does not imply that natural laws do not operate in the miracle situation and that natural forces, elevated by a superior power, cannot contribute to the miraculous effect. A transcendent intervention may make use of the proper

powers of nature. God may, for example, accelerate the
natural healing processes, so that an instantaneous cure takes
place, but which follows certain natural laws. *Some* miracles can be so explained. Dhanis admits too that a lively
faith in God may merit God's action: and it may also adopt
the subject of the miraculous cure to be the earthly point
of insertion for God's miraculous action.

Dhanis concedes also that many cannot accept the notion
of a miracle as an exception to natural laws; for they think
that this would be to deprive the universe of order. But
there exist various orders in the universe, hierarchically organized, and the orders of ethical and religious realities,
and of grace, are superior to the order of nature. An exception to the inferior order is still a part of the total order.

One of the reasons frequently alleged for passing over in
silence the notion of an exception to the laws of nature
is the difficulty of knowing them fully. Dhanis argues
that *in certain circumstances* we can know them sufficiently
to make a judgment concerning an exception. If the prodigy
is exceptional, contrary to the usual course of nature observed in many and varied situations, if it is free from weird
or artificial elements engendering the suspicion that new
and artificial factors are at work, and if one is aware of no
other such phenomena in secular circumstances then one
may know that he is face to face with an exception to
natural laws.[21]

Dhanis believes that the number and variety of circumstances in which an extraordinary event is realized and the
normal environment in which it takes place tend to exclude
the possibility that it is attributable to the operation of some
unknown natural factor. The fact that we do not know of

similar prodigies in secular or pagan situations persuades us that the event is not simply a case of an exceptional collaboration of known laws of nature. The exceptions to the known laws of nature will not surpass certain limits; they will not fulfill the above-mentioned three conditions.

Dhanis doubts that one can sacrifice the physical transcendence of a miracle—its exception to natural laws—without weakening the certitude derived from miracles. Such a precision from physical transcendence would also, in his opinion, be less consonant with tradition. The Vatican Council, for example, had distinguished miracles and prophecies, one of which reveals the omnipotence of God and the other the divine knowledge; both of these, miracles and prophecy, are most certain signs of divine revelation. But if one takes the approach of certain authors, both miracles and prophecy would be recognizable because of their transcendence *as signs*, authentic signs from God in a providentially arranged religious context. This, however, would not result in two *distinct* types of divine intervention: of power and of knowledge, but would rather manifest one object: God intervening by prudence to arrange the meeting of extraordinary events with religious circumstances and context. It appears that the Vatican Council implied more than that in distinguishing the effects of God's omnipotence and His omniscience.[22]

Dhanis admits, however, that the Vatican Council did not intend to propose the physical transcendence of a miracle as an object of *faith*. It appears to him, however, that the mind of the Council demonstrates that the sign value of a miracle is at least highly guaranteed by its physical transcendence, although the Council does not necessarily imply that one can *only* discern a miracle as such if one takes this transcendence into account. It seems to us that Dhanis' case rests primarily upon his rational arguments to establish that one who prescinds from the physical transcendence of a miracle has no certain basis left for recognizing a miracle as such. If one admits physical transcendence one has a certain norm for stating that this particular prodigy in this religious context is a sign from God. If one does not admit such transcendence, how can one be sure?

In 1906 Abbé Bros, supporting and developing the ideas of Blondel, had proposed a method for discerning a miracle without appeal to physical transcendence. Like Blondel, Bros did not believe that a miracle could be defined simply by its transcendence of natural laws.[23] The reason for his position was the classic objection: we can never be sure when a fact does transcend natural laws since we do not know everything about natural laws. Moreover, a miracle may well take place when the event *is naturally achievable*, but the context and sign value point to God's intervention. Bros suggested as a norm for recognition of a miracle the theory of "constant coincidents." The extraordinary, baffling and wonderful events all take place in such a context that we can with safety declare that God has intervened. These events bear the mark of the supernatural; their religious characteristics, the circumstances in which they occur, manifest God as the common antecedent. The constant factor is the evident religious connection pointing to God. Seeing the event in its totality we can only conclude that the author of the event is God. Scientific apologetics can then identify a miracle by applying the method of constant coincidents. Through elimination of all the variable and accidental circumstances it discovers one that is constant.

There are, moreover, necessary dispositions of a moral order before one can read aright the sign that is a miracle. An interior spiritual preparation is needed—not faith, for that would be a vicious circle—but at least a receptivity to religious matters, a willingness to believe, if it appears rational and prudent, and an openness to the truth.

Dhanis criticizes this method by pointing out that in the ultimate analysis, if it is to give certitude, it must depend upon a recognition of that physical transcendence which its authors reject or consider useless. He submits that a coincidence of context and prodigy, if found in only one instance, would be of little significance. Here we disagree with him. Even one instance, given the proper dispositions in the viewer and a fortunate set of circumstances, should awaken more than the suspicion that the event is owing to chance.[24]

One should really, he continues, consider several or many prodigies of different types. But even this would not suffice, for if one could discover similar cases, even imperfectly similar, in secular surroundings, the argument would prove nothing. One would be reduced to those miracles which verify the note of transcendence of natural laws and *it is this* which lies at the basis of the theory of constant coincidents.

The theory of constant coincidents should be valid for the future, if it is so for the present and the past. But it cannot prove that Providence must in the future assure that at no point in history can there be similar prodigies in secular situations. The only firm basis of such a proof, Dhanis believes, would be the irreducibility of such prodigies to the laws of nature.[25] This argument seems to us weak. In the classic theory Providence assures us that a physically transcendent miracle will not be worked in confirmation of a false doctrine or religion. Why not invoke it also to assure that prodigies will not take place in profane circumstances? If the theorists of context coincidents cannot appeal to Providence to ensure that prodigies do not occur in a profane context, why should the classical theorists appeal to God's wisdom and goodness not to lead man into error through confirming by a miracle a false religion? Moreover, the question of a profane context is not precisely what is at issue. If the constant coincidents theory is correct, prodigies in a secular context would not even be examined for miraculous properties. The religious nature of the context is intrinsic to the prodigy, whether the religion be false or true. Once you demand a religious context it appears to us that Providence can be legitimately appealed to.

There is perhaps a certain obscurity which prevents our understanding of the relationship between physical miracles and physical laws. In order to throw light on the matter W. H. Nicholls wrote his article "Physical Laws and Physical Miracles."[26] Nicholls claims that our confusion results chiefly from an overemphasis on the aspect of a miracle as an exception to physical law. Theologians claim that the principle of sufficient reason demands the positive intervention of God as the only possible explanation for the miraculous physical event. In his article Nicholls shows that that is not necessarily the case.

A physical law is defined as intelligibility immanent in the uniform activity of bodies. Denial of the fact that physical laws do exist outside the mind and outside the senses inevitably leads to sheer skepticism. That some physical laws are certain, is obvious, as for example, "A grown man *generally* cannot walk on an unfrozen lake." There are, of course, various types of physical laws—determinate and statistical, unverifiable and empirically verifiable.

A determinate law describes single events which are assigned a probability of one or zero and which can be recognized by words such as "always" or "never." For example: at ordinary pressure, water always expands upon freezing.[27]

A statistical law describes events or a number of sets of events by assigning to them fractional probabilities, using the words *"generally," "rarely."* For example: according to statistical mechanics, under stated conditions of temperature and pressure the probability that a man can walk on a lake for ten seconds is one in $10^{10,000,000,000}$.

Now a physical miracle is defined as a physical, extraordinary observable event of Divine authorship. To be recognized as such it must occur in a religious context and be so extraordinary that God's intervention is certain.

A religious context is had when there is a positive absence of the devil's work and a positive reference to God. An example would be the raising of Lazarus, an act which the principle of sufficient reason moves our mind to accept as miraculous.

The raising of Lazarus is also a physically extraordinary event, having reference to a verifiable physical law which is statistical, objective and certain. People who have apparently died and have been buried for three days have a *vanishingly small probability* of returning to life. As long as this law speaks of "vanishingly small" probability rather than of a probability, the event is an *exception*, not a violation of a physical law.

A miracle, however, such as that of Peter walking on the water does not seem to be an exception to any verifiable physical law. Without a religious context, this event is inexplicable except in terms of an exceedingly improbable statistical freak within the laws of statistical mechanics (one in $10,^{10,000,000,000}$). This might seem merely a chance event within the laws of nature but the religious context is the clue needed to explain the miracle satisfactorily. The human mind could never be satisfied with a mere scientific explanation of the infinitisimal, nonzero probability of someone saying, "Come," and Peter's action of walking on the water. The religious context, not the existential skeleton of the incident, frees the mind of doubt and gives certitude to the intellect. It is a case of common sense, not modern science, and of a religious context intimately joined with a physical event.[28]

The certain recognition of the miraculous, then, does not depend on our knowledge of physical laws, or even on the recognition of a strict exception to any verifiable physical law. These are not necessary for a highly improbable case within a statistical framework can *under suitable circumstances* be recognized as a miracle. Such, at least, is the opinion of Fr. Nicholls, who points out that to claim that we can prove that a given event contradicts the laws of nature would seem nonsense to a scientist. Our knowledge of nature is too meager. A scientist would admit that Peter's walking on the waters was extraordinary, but would add that modern science does not exclude the possibility but merely reduces the probability to the vanishing point. The fact that a grown man cannot walk on an unfrozen lake is only statistical law, but it is certainly true, it can be empirically checked, it is verifiable. However even if *all* physical laws were of this variety we could recognize a miracle when the vanishingly small probability occurs, *if the religious context and sign value were to be taken into consideration*. The raising of Lazarus demonstrates the same point. It cannot be simply an improbably statistical freak in the precise *context* in which it occurs. In other words it is not necessary to verify the presence of an *exception* to some certainly known physical law in order to recognize a miracle. Nicholls believes that miracles do confront us with the evidence of a special divine causality expressing itself as a violation of some, perhaps *unverifiable*, physical law, but that it is not necessary to recognize a violation of a *certainly* known physical law to declare that a miracle is present.

Modern science seems generally to accept the fact that all scientific laws are not sufficiently known to establish with certainty what is beyond the powers of nature. The scientific investigation of miracles has been made more difficult by the transition from a deterministic viewpoint of the universe to one which looks on the laws of nature as statistical. One type of statistical theory prevalent today deals with large numbers of observable events, and furnishes a difficulty to the theory of miracles in that it allows for the concept of fluctuations. Fluctuations are improbable, but *possible;* no deviation from the law is outside the scope of the theory. The laws of probability simply make exceptions unlikely. Hence the scientist, when confronted with a baffling event, does not see this as an *exception* to the law, but as one included, with a very slight degree of probability, in the law itself. He is aware that his knowledge of the laws of nature is incomplete and hence his reaction is not likely to be that the startling event is impossible.

A second type of statistical theory in vogue today is that of quantum mechanics, a highly intricate mathematical formalism developed largely in the third decade of this century. While the first type of statistical theory deals with the behavior of systems composed of large numbers of particles, quantum mechanics deals with the behavior of individual microscopic particles. It is basic to this theory that a statement made about an individual particle or event must be stated in the language of probability. A quantum mechanics law can tell us only what will probably happen in any given case. This gives added strength to the objection to miracles taken from statistical theories; how can we state that something is contrary to the laws of nature if the laws of nature give us only probabilities?[29]

In conclusion we may attempt to summarize the varying positions of Catholic theologians today on the subject of miracles. Certain theologians believe that a miracle is physically transcendent, that it can be known as such with certainty and *without* appeal to its seismological transcendence. Others believe that it is hardly ever possible to *prove* physical transcendence and that this element is not needed in the definition; thus the question as to whether or not a miracle is *de facto* physically transcendent is relatively unimportant. Others believe that a miracle is physically transcendent and should be so defined but that this trancendence cannot be known aside from the seismological transcendence. Hence as regards the knowability of a miracle, the element of physical transcendence can and should be underplayed. It is sufficient to establish the existence of a divine sign without entering into the question as to whether the event is caused by a direct intervention of God or by His providential arranging of the joining of context and prodigy. Finally, some have suggested that God might have from the beginning foreseen and planned a statistical fluctuation to take place in a definite context and that this fluctuation, *in accordance with* natural statistical law, is sufficient for a miracle.

It should be obvious that the recent insistence upon the total context and sign value of a miracle is an improvement over the more rationalistic position which had become generally accepted in manuals of theology. Almost all writers on the subject of miracles agree on this. Dhanis, who does not believe that the sign value is necessary to discern physical transcendence, has nevertheless provided one of the most illuminating analyses of miracle as sign. A considerable time will probably have to elapse before a final judgment can be given on these various theories. The area of disagreement is not so large as it may appear at first glance and in some cases what appears new is a return to a position which is highly biblical and traditional. Augustine had emphasized the biblical concept of miracle as a divine sign. He would no doubt have appreciated the contributions of Pascal, Newman, and Scheler to an analysis of the subjective attitudes required for a real understanding of miracle. Those writers who stress the total context of a miracle are certainly close to the biblical notion of a miracle as an invitation on the part of God, a message addressed from one Person to another in the encounter of faith. The re-integration of the notions of context, sign value, spiritual preparedness in the discussion of miracle makes it evident that Catholic theology is gaining balance and complete-ness in its treatment of miracles. The present-day treat-ment is thoroughly biblical. There did exist at one time the danger of one-sidedness in an approach to miracles simply as physically transcendent, when controversy with deter-minists and deists urged theologians to devote most of their attention to this aspect.

In the opinion of this author dogmatic tradition per-suades to the view that a miracle *is* physically transcendent, without imposing such a position as a matter of faith. However, the arguments used to prove that one can estab-lish this physical transcendence independently of the re-ligious context do not appear to me convincing. It seems that a prodigy which is an exception to physical laws from the statistical, if not from the metaphysical viewpoint, and which is an effect of Providence can be in certain contexts unmistakably recognized as a divine sign, whether or not one calls this a miracle in the strict sense. Again, whether a prodigy is caused by a *direct* intervention of God or by His mediate causality can be left an open question. In practice, as regards the *knowability* of a miracle, it seems to me a well-nigh impossible position to attempt to prove physical transcendence apart from the total context. If one *can* establish physical transcendence it will be only with the assistance lent to us by the total context.

When recent theologians speak of dispositions required for the recognition of a miracle they are not implying that faith is one of them. But some appreciation of the supernatural quality of the sign seems to be demanded and a recognition that man must have an openness to religious truth together with an initial desire (not exigency) for a closer supernatural relationship with God which will open the mind to a higher order of reality than the natural. Grace can and does arouse in man a longing, howsoever vague, for that supernatural destiny to which man is *de facto* called. We believe that in the ordinary course of events this grace is operative in enabling man to discern in the miracle what it is—a sign of the supernatural world to which God invites him.

Fr. Liégé has aptly described the complex reality that is signified by a miracle: "As an extraordinary and beneficient event, it reveals the God of grace and of fatherly tenderness; as an act of healing it announces spiritual salvation; as an historical event it manifests the entrance of God into history. In brief, its whole significance bears witness to the coming of the Kingdom, the presence of God who vivifies and saves, who has pity on the human condition: it announces the Gospel."[30]

In the early part of the twentieth century Modernism and liberal criticism tended to reject miracles as absurd. Today the situation has changed. There is a growing interest in exceptional phenomena which in some cases has progressed so far as to degenerate into irrational desire for the marvelous in religion.[31]

As Catholics we must remember two important points 1) the traditional Christian view of miracles; 2) the final discerning of miracles is the prerogative of the Church.

The documents on which our Christian faith rest do contain a miraculous element. Deeds are attributed to Christ which are not considered normal. These are called marvels which cause wonder and awe because one meets in them something inexplicable of which God is maintained to be the cause. In these events God appears to work beyond the order of secondary causes, or if secondary causes are used, the effect seems to be beyond their ordinary capacity.

It is impossible to eliminate miracles from the Gospels for the sacred authors are convinced that there exist miraculous events performed by Christ by means of supranormal powers which show His union with the Father. Miracles can be denied only by saying that the gospels are not historical.

However, the gospel writers do not list miracles for their own sake but rather as signs that point beyond themselves and draw our attention to something else. St. Mark uses them to indicate that God is at work in Christ to support His claim as Messias and Son of God; St. John, to indicate the glory of God present in the salvific work of Christ.

Miracles are acts in which God's salvific purpose is revealed. They are prodigies in which God intervenes directly or makes use of secondary causes to reveal His purpose. They are not *lawless violations* of natural order but rather a sign of a higher order, that of God's freely offered healing and elevating grace.

Miracles must always be recognized for what they really are—signs. The full significance of miraculous events dawns only on the mind that is illuminated by goodwill and drawn by grace. Miracles are objective but it is only with the power of the Holy Ghost that their *full* meaning as signs can be grasped.[32]

NOTES

1. C. Tresmontant, *Etudes de métaphysique biblique*, Paris, 1955, pp. 223-228.

2. H. Knight, "The Old Testament concept of miracle," *Scottish Journal of Theology* (1952), 335.

3. E. Jacob, *Theology of the Old Testament*, New York, 1955, pp. 223-235.

4. A. Lefèvre, "Miracle," *Dictionaire de la Bible, Supplément*, col. 1301.

5. B. Anderson, *Understanding the Old Testament*, Englewood Cliffs, N. J., 1957, pp. 43-49.

6. H. Robinson, "The nature miracles of the Old Testament," *Journal of Theological Studies* (1944), 1.

7. P. Menoud, "Miracle et sacrement dans le Nouveau Testament," *Verbum Caro*, 1952, 142, Cf. J. Benoit "La divinité de Jésus Christ dans les Evangiles Synoptiques, *Lumière et Vie* (1953), 43-74, and L. Cerfaux, "Temoins du Christ, *Angelicum* (1943), 166-183.

8. W. Carroll, "St. Augustine's preaching on Miracles," *Homiletic and Pastoral Review* (1948), 755-762. See also: P. De Vooght, "La notion philosophique du miracle selon S. Augustin," *Recherches de théologie ancienne et médiévale* (1938), 317-343 and "La théologie du miracle selon Saint Augustin, *Recherches de théologie ancienne et mediévale* (1939), 197-222.

9. J. Hardon, "The concept of miracle from St. Augustine to Modern Apologetics," *Theological Studies* (1954), 229-257. and K. McNamara "The nature and recognition of miracles," *Irish Theological Quarterly* (1960), 301-302.

10. J. Hardon, *art. cit.* 235-245. Cf. A. van Hove, *La doctrine du miracle chez. S. Thomas et son accord avec les principes de la recherche scientifique*, Paris, 1927.

11. J. Hardon, *art cit.*, 247.

12. L. de Grandmaison, *Jesus-Christ*, Paris, 1928, Vol. II, pp. 225-255. Cf. A. Liégé, "Reflexions théologiques sur le miracle" in *Pensée scientifique et foi chrétienne*, Paris (1953), 206-218; also E. Masure,

"Le miracle comme signe," *Revue de sciences philosophiques et théologiques* (1959), 274 ff; D. Dubarle "L'attitude du savant chrétien en face du fait merveilleux," *Lumière et Vie* (1957), 321-350.

13. E. Dhanis, "Qu'est-ce qu'un miracle?" *Gregorianum* (1959), 201-241.

14. V. Marcozzi, "Il Miracolo," in *Problemi e Orientamenti di Teologia Dommatica*, Milan (1957), 108-109.

15. M. de Locht, "Maurice Blondel et sa controverse au sujet du miracle," *Ephemerides theologicae Lovanienses* (1954), 344-390.

16. G. de Broglie, *Pour une théorie rationalle de l'acte de foi*, Part II, Paris, 1948, pp. 43-51.

17. *Ibid.*, pp. 51-54.

18. M. Blondel, *L'Action*, Paris, 1893, pp. 392-398. Cf. *Annales de philosophie chrétienne*, 1895-1896, pp. 337-346; 466-482; 599-616; 131-147; 255-267; 338-350; also A. Lalande, *Vocabulaire technique et critique de la philosophie*, Vol. I, pp. 469-471. See also P. De Locht, "Maurice Blondel et sa controverse au sujet du miracle," *Ephemerides theologicae Lovanienses* (1954), 344-390 and B. Welte, "Maurice Blondel," *Theologische Revue* (1955), 5-12.

19. F. Taymans "Le miracle, signe du surnature," *Nouvelle revue théologique* (1955), 222-245. For a full discussion of the importance of context see L. Monden, *Le Miracle signe du salut*, Paris, 1959.

20. E. Dhanis, "Qu'est-ce qu'un miracle?" *Gregorianum* (1959, 201-241; See also Dhanis, "Un chaînon de la preuve du miracle," in *Problemi scelti di teologia contemporanea* (Analecta Gregoriana 68) Rome, 1954, 66-70.

21. Dhanis, "Qu'est-ce qu'un miracle?" 213-214.

22. *Ibid*, 219-224.

23. A. Bros, "Comment constater le miracle?" *Annales de philosophie chrétienne* (1906), 250-267.

24. Dhanis, "Qu'est-ce qu'un miracle?" 225.

25. *Ibid*, 227.

26. W. Nicholls, "Physical laws and physical miracles" *Irish Theological Quarterly* (1960), 49-56.

27. *Ibid.*

28. *Ibid.*

29. J. Carter "Theological recognition of Miracles," *Theological Studies* (1959), 175-197.

30. P. Liégé, "Le miracle dans la theologie catholique," *Lumière et Vie* (1957), 79.

It is of interest to note that the Protestant attitude to miracles has undergone an evolution in this century. See A. Fridrichsen, *Le Problème du miracle dans le christianisme primitif*, Strasbourg, 1925; F. Torrance, *Expository Studies in St. John's Miracles*, London, 1938; A. Richardson, *The Miracle Stories of the Gospels*, London, 1941 and G. Marquardt, *Das Wunderproblem in der Deutschen protestantischen Theologie der Gegenwart*, 1933. Protestant theology after the First World War, with some exceptions, tends to approach the Catholic positions on miracles.

31. I. Hislop, "Miracles and the gospels," *Blackfriars* (1958), 57-60.

Thomas E. Clarke

>>>><<<<<

SOME ASPECTS OF
CURRENT CHRISTOLOGY

It is an unfortunate, though perhaps inevitable, feature of contemporary theology that the Christ of apologetics is more prominent than the Christ of dogmatics. Concern for relating the Jesus of history to the Christ of Faith, or, to employ more current categories, for integrating the *historisch* and *geschichtlich* elements of the Christ-reality, has overshadowed some excellent work of the past decade in the field of dogmatic Christology. The present essay is an attempt to present a few of the more significant contributions in this field. It is far from being comprehensive, and is confined, for the most part, to Catholic authors. Leaving aside the problems of soteriological and cosmic Christology, it will focus on questions more immediately connected with the dogma of Chalcedon. Even here it will do little more than sample a very extensive literature.[1]

I

We may begin with a simple statement of Karl Adam: "The mystery of Christ does not lie in the fact that he is God, but that he is God-man."[2] The central problem of dogmatic Christology may be described as the problem of the-one-and-the-many in Christ. It is the task of Christology to inquire in what sense, to what degree, under what conditions, to what purpose, with what consequences, are God and man somehow uniquely one in Christ Jesus. This Christological inquiry, in its historical aspect, is largely a tale of two cities, Alexandria and Antioch, considered not merely as two rival theological schools of the fourth and fifth centuries, but as two enduring approaches to the mystery of Christ, rooted in two religious mentalities, each with a special sensitivity to that aspect of the God-man which the other mentality leaves somewhat in the shade. We may look at the clash and blend of these two approaches in three phases, patristic, scholastic, modern, or, otherwise expressed, positive, speculative, psychological.

First, considerable attention is being given today to the Christology of ancient Alexandria and Antioch. The Alexandrian Christology is described as a "descending," or *logos-sarx*, Christology. It begins not with the man Jesus but with the eternal Word. Under the influence especially of the Stoic notion of the *logos* as the unique, immanent, hegemonic and vivifying principle in man, Alexandria tends to conceive the eternal Word as assuming the role of this *logos* in Christ. The advantages and disadvantages of such an approach are apparent. The unity of Christ is safeguarded, but at the risk of denying or neglecting the existence, or at least the redemptive significance, of the human mind and will of Christ. One prominent, though controverted, trend today is to stress the limitations rather than the advantages of this approach. In particular Saints Athanasius and Cyril, the two great champions of Alexandrian Christology, are considered by some to have failed to give to the human soul of Christ its due place in their soteriology. One might use the phrase, "functional Apollinarism," except that there is question not of positive error but of an understandable inability to exploit this facet of the reality of the God-man.[3]

Discussion of the virtues and defects of the Antiochene school is also part of the present scene. Antiochene Christology is described as "ascending," because it begins with the man Jesus, especially as portrayed in the Synoptics. The phrase *assumptus homo* expresses what is characteristic of this approach: a true, complete man has been assumed by the Word. Opposition to Alexandria is conveyed by the formula: *logos-anthropos*. In Christ the Word and a man are intimately united. Whereas in earlier decades the focus of interest in the Antiochene school was Nestorius, today it is his master Theodore of Mopsuestia who is the central figure. Theodore in his own day was a great champion of orthodoxy against the extreme *logos-sarx* Christology of Apollinaris. Two centuries later he was condemned as a heretic by the Fifth Ecumenical Council. What judgment is to be made today of Theodore? Francis Sullivan concluded in his doctoral dissertation that Theodore was truly the father of Nestorianism.[4] John McKenzie, among others, has challenged this verdict.[5] The dispute has more than technical or antiquarian interest. It was no accident that the school of Antioch, and Theodore in particular, should stress the reality and value of the rational and human in the Word Incarnate. For this is exactly what Antioch did in its approach to the word of God in Scripture. Theodore was the champion of literal exegesis in his own day, and is somewhat the darling of exegetes today. Nor was it an accident that Alexandria, more mystical in its Christology, should be mystical also in its approach to Scripture. And so quite apart from the technical questions involved, it is perfectly natural to hear Father McKenzie, that vigorous exponent of critical exegesis and critic of Origenian hermeneutics, speaking out in defense of Theodore. Just as it was natural for Cardinal Newman, whose theory of the mystical sense of Scripture is more Alexandrian, to characterize Antioch as the very metropolis of heresy.[6]

There is a point here of some significance for the religious life of the student of Christology, whether in seminary, college, or armchair. It is that the conflict which led to Ephesus and Chalcedon involved something more than strong personalities or Church-State politics or linguistic niceties or philosophical subtleties. It was a question—and still is—of religious temperament and attitude and experience, which will influence theological positions and in turn be influenced by them. We accept this idea quite readily in the question of predestination, grace, and freedom, but perhaps we have not paid enough attention to its importance in Christology. The study of the God-man is not only a way of finding out something about Him. Like the study of grace and freedom, it is an excellent instrument for telling us something about ourselves. Most of us tend to be Monophysites or Nestorians, Thomists or Scotists, in Christology, with implications that are not purely academic.

Leaving aside other aspects of the ancient Christologies, for example, the influence of the West at Chalcedon, something must be said about the scholastic version of the ageless Alexandria-Antioch debate. Here the principal question being discussed is the question of a created existence in Christ. It is well known that the so-called ecstasy of existence theory, which denied the presence in Christ of any created *esse*, has been in favor with Thomists generally, whether of the Cajetan school or among the followers of Cardinal Billot. Father de la Taille's theory of created actuation left room for a created existential reality which he was willing to call a secondary human *esse*. But for the most part Thomists have insisted on the illation: *unum ens ergo unum esse*, and have felt that it imposed the so-called ecstasy of existence idea. They have defended this as the view of St. Thomas. This opinion was weakened in its historical foundations by the conclusion of Pelster and others, that the *Quaestio de Unione Verbi Incarnati* is not only authentic but a late work of Aquinas, and that in it he espouses a twofold existence. More significantly, some prominent Thomists of the Cajetan viewpoint, notably Dom Diepen, a Benedictine writing in the *Revue Thomiste*, and Jacques Maritain, who admits that Dom Diepen's critique of the ecstasy of existence theory has caused him to abandon his own previous position, now acknowledge the presence in Christ of a created *esse*. The discussion is rather subtle, intricate, even perhaps esoteric. Here again, however, it would be a mistake to miss its religious implications. The Thomist Christology is admittedly more Alexandrian than Antiochene, especially by contrast with those of Scotus and Suarez. The effect of the positions of Diepen and Maritain is to place them, on the spectrum of Christological conception, somewhat closer to center than the proponents of the ecstasy of existence theory, and to reflect a greater concern than previously for the distinct reality of the humanity of Christ. If one recalls the care which Maritain takes, in such works as *True Humanism*, to give to the temporal order its proper measure of autonomy, the general consistency of his thought becomes apparent.[7]

As we would expect in an age which is engrossed with psychology, personal existence, the subject, Alexandria and Antioch meet today in a concern for the conscious life of the man Jesus. Protestant theologians have for a long time attempted to express the mystery of Christ, especially in what regards the Pauline Kenosis, in psychological terms. But apart from Rosmini, Günther and the effort to refute them in the nineteenth century, Catholic theologians till a few decades ago were less interested in this aspect of Christology. It was the second edition of Paul Galtier's *L'unité du Christ* in 1939 which stimulated reflection on the psychological unity of Christ, especially in terms of the question: how was our Lord humanly aware of His own divinity.[8]

The probing response of Galtier to the question was quite in keeping with his position, substantially that of

Scotus and Tiphanus, on the ontological structure of Christ. Since, he reasoned, the hypostatic union is a pure relation to the Word of an existing human nature, since the Word has no causal influence, either efficient or quasiformal, peculiar to Himself, on His own humanity and its activities, since human consciousness reaches the person only through the mediation of the nature, which alone is the formal eliciting principle of operation, it follows that Christ has no strict human consciousness of His divinity. He does have human knowledge of His divinity, thanks to the beatific vision, which preserves Him from the error of affirming a human person. But, says Galtier, this is an objective knowledge, not a knowledge of the subject as such, hence not strictly a consciousness. Galtier's position is strongly Antiochene, in that both ontologically and psychologically it is more concerned with the distinct reality of the humanity of Christ and its consubstantiality with our humanity than with the unity of Christ and the unique role of the Word in the life of this one particular human being. The Word influences the life of His own humanity only in common with the Father and the Holy Spirit.

At the opposite extreme from this position we may perhaps place the position of Xiberta, which for some critics comes too close to Eutycheanism for comfort. Xiberta speaks of a radical sublimation and supernaturalization of the humanity of Christ by the hypostatic union, leaving in the humanity effects which can be perceived by human consciousness.[9]

Perhaps we may express the dilemma somewhat as follows: On the one hand it would seem that Christ, as a man, as the perfect man, should have a true human consciousness of His own divine self. On the other hand, since consciousness reaches the subject, the person, only insofar as the person or subject is present to itself in its own operation, it does not seem possible for an infinite subject to be reached consciously and as subject in actions which are finite and which proceed from a finite formal principle. In the human self awareness of Christ, the subject who is self-aware is infinite, divine, but the awareness itself is finite, human, with a structure consubstantial with our self-awareness.

Between the positions of Galtier and Xiberta a wide variety of opinions exists, differing both in their metaphysical presuppositions and in their analysis of human consciousness. There are those who maintain that the problem as placed above is a false one.[10] It would appear that today a good number of theologians are favoring a position which is, in a sense, *a via media*, and, in another sense, represents a new insight: Christ's full human self-awareness is impossible without recourse to the beatific vision, which, however, should not be understood as a purely objective viewing of the Godhead; in Christ it is also knowledge of the subject as such or at least it stands in intimate relation with this knowledge, so that neither is intelligible without the other. Some go further and attempt to break through a certain dichotomy between the ontological and the psychological which may be at the root of the dilemma. According to this view, knowledge, self-awareness, self-possession, self-disposition, is not a mere adornment or refinement of being, it is being itself, in its fullness. Where being exists in its perfection, in God, it is identically infinite knowledge, infinite self-awareness. And in the hierarchy of creation, the same is true. To be in any full sense is to know, to be aware of self. To be a man is to be aware of oneself as a man. To be humanly the God-man is to be humanly aware of oneself as the God-man. Hence, says Karl Rahner, in virtue of the hypostatic union itself, the human soul of Christ is immediately and consciously in the Word, and the beatific vision is merely the consequence of this consciousness; it is the hypostatic union itself insofar as the hypostatic union is necessarily an *intelligible actu* in the *intelligens actu* of the human soul of Christ. It is the prolongation, if you will, of the hypostatic union in the sphere of intelligence, the knowledge situation connatural with natural divine sonship.[11]

Something should be said also of current opinion on the related question of the human knowledge of Christ in general. There would appear to be a growing uneasiness with the teaching, as commonly understood since St. Thomas, of a triple human knowledge in Christ, beatific, infused, experiential. Particularly obnoxious to many today is the tendency of past ages to extend the object of Christ's infused knowledge to include areas having nothing directly to do with salvation.[12] Moreover, the theological principle of perfection, which insists on attributing to Christ in His human pilgrimage all the intellectual endowments of angels and men, is being closely scrutinized. How can we do justice to the condition of Christ as *homo viator*, as like to us in all save sin, as subject of a *kenosis*, as learning obedience by what He suffered (Heb. 5:8), as ignorant of the day of judgment (Matt. 24:36), if for the sake of an abstract principle we burden His human mind in its earthly pilgrimage with types and degrees of knowledge which would appear to have no clearly established soteriological function, which are with difficulty compatible with one another, and which run the danger of reducing the *kenosis* to a purely ontological reality? Moreover, it has been suggested that the principle of perfection, which is quite in place where there is question of moral excellence, was applied to the realm of intellectual excellence by Augustine and others under the influence of a certain Socratic notion that knowledge is virtue. So runs the negative critique. The positive attempts at reconciling what we might call the principle of perfection and the principle of imperfection have focused on the beatific vision and on infused knowledge. As regards the beatific vision, there is first of all the desire to stress the differences rather than the points in common between the immediate vision of God had by the blessed and the immediate vision had by Christ as *viator*. In fact, it has been suggested that not all immediate vision is beatific. The immediate effects of the vision of God are conditioned by the state of the subject. A soul in hell would be tormented, not beatified, by an immediate vision of God. The vision as had by Christ in His mortal, kenotic condition is to be analogously understood. Also with regard to the knowledge of vision, some have gone back to St. Bonaventure for the idea that the vision of all created reality in God was not always actual for the human mind of Christ; a habitual vision sufficed (Karl Adam has gone further and has said "potential"). In this view the ignorance of the day of judgment which Our Lord attributes to Himself is taken to mean: Not even in His knowledge of immediate vision did He have *actual* knowledge of the day of judgment. Such an actual knowledge did not belong to the mission of revelation and salvation given to Christ by His Father.

This tendency to reduce the scope of knowledge of vision is accompanied by a similar tendency regarding infused knowledge. Some theologians today reject the thesis of the presence of infused ideas in the human mind of Christ from the very beginning of His life. They feel that whatever value tradition has given to the doctrine of infused knowledge can be saved by making it consist in a certain supernatural illumination whose role is to "translate," so to speak, the knowledge of vision into the sphere of the communicable and revealable, and thus integrate knowledge of vision with experiential knowledge.

While it would be misleading to attempt a simple correlation of these current views on the psychological unity and knowledge of Christ with patristic and scholastic positions, it may perhaps be said that the attempt now in progress to assure for Christ a true and full experience of the human situation, even as regards intellectual limitations, represents Antioch more than Alexandria. It may be significant that St. Bonaventure rather than St. Thomas has provided one of the key ideas utilized in this effort.[13]

II

So far we have been concerned with the content of the mystery of Christ, the verification on various levels of the one-and-many. A very important aspect of current Christology is concerned with the form in which this content is expressed, and especially with the relationship of the conciliar form, as exemplified in the definition of Chalcedon, with the biblical form. Chalcedon spoke of Christ as a single divine person in two distinct natures. It terminated its definition by stating that this teaching was in accord with what the prophets and our Lord Himself had taught. But when we turn to Scripture, even to the New Testament, do we find there Chalcedon's doctrine of nature and person? And if not, how are we to look upon Chalcedon? A betrayal? An irrelevancy? A Hellenization of the Gospel? An extension of revelation, legitimate or illegitimate?

The question is, of course, not a new one, but it has entered a new phase, owing especially to Oscar Cullmann's book, *The Christology of the New Testament*.[14] While his work belongs properly to the realm of exegesis and biblical theology rather than that of dogmatics, it does indulge in a few generalizations of a doctrinal nature which have caused some exegetes and theologians, both Catholic and Protestant, to question the orthodoxy of Cullmann's views. A later article by the author has served to remove a good deal of the misunderstanding.[15] But, quite apart from the question of orthodoxy, the statements in question serve to highlight the problem of the relationship of the Church's dogma of the Incarnation to the New Testament statements about Christ. This is our reason for dealing with the question here.

Cullmann's book is a masterful presentation of New Testament Christology in terms of the names and titles of Christ, arranged in four classes, those related respectively to His earthly life (prophet, suffering servant, high priest), His future life (Messiah, Son of Man), His present life (Lord, Saviour), His preexistent life (logos, Son of God, God). In addition to his opinions on exegetical details Cullmann has a more general proposition (which, however, he is careful to qualify). It is that, whereas Chalcedon was concerned with the being of Christ, what He is, His divine and human nature, His single person, the New Testament is concerned with the work of Christ, what He does, His salvific function. New Testament Christology is functional, not ontological. These two types of statement correspond respectively to Semitic and Hellenic modes of thought. Even where the New Testament speaks of the Son of God prior to the Incarnation and prior to creation (and Cullmann admits that it does), it speaks of Him under the aspect of function, not of nature. It is not concerned with whether He is one substance or nature with the Father, or whether His being is a being derived from the Father.

This is by no means an adequate presentation of the thesis of functional Christology (if it can be called a thesis and not a tendency), in which Cullmann finds a large measure of agreement among some Catholics, notably the Benedictine exegete Jacques Dupont and the Dominican exegete M. E. Boismard. On the Anglican side Dom Gregory Dix had already voiced a similar view in his little book *Jew and Greek*.[16] Without going into too much detail, it may be helpful to indicate what kind of problem, if any, is raised here for dogmatic theologians, and how we may best profit by Cullmann's idea.

First of all, it should be noted that Cullmann himself, both in his book and in his later article, qualifies his thesis on New Testament functionalism. He does not completely exclude nonfunctional statements about Christ. In the *Choisir* article he acknowledges two passages (John 1:1; I Cor. 15:28) which explicitly mention the being of Christ anterior to creation and consequent upon the fulfillment of salvation history. Moreover, he is willing to admit a certain historical necessity and even legitimacy in the development from a functional to an ontological Christology. He does not condemn Chalcedon. Yet in other passages (somewhat inconsistently, it seems) he speaks as if the New Testament Christology is exclusively functional, and speaks somewhat pejoratively of the development of an ontological Christology.[17] This same regret over the transition from Semitic to Hellenic modes of expression appeared in at least one of his earlier works, where he portrays the regrettable process by which the Trinitarian confession replaced the more primitive Christological confession.[18] There is the added difficulty that functional Christology has not been very sharply defined by Cullmann, and can mean several things. It can mean that the salvific work of Christ, rather than the being of Christ, is of primary interest to the New Testament authors. It can mean that the New Testament never (or hardly ever) speaks of the being of Christ without relating it to His activity. It can mean that the authors, being Semites, were incapable of conceiving Christ in terms of nature or person, and this either in a technical philosophical sense or in a popular sense available to the ordinary man of today. It can mean, finally, and more radically, that the Christian revelation, contained in its totality in Scripture, or at least communicated to mankind exclusively through Semitic minds, has nothing explicitly or implicitly to say of the being of Christ (or for that matter, of God).

The first observation therefore is that there would appear to be a certain ambiguity, inconsistency, and vagueness present in Cullmann's formulation of his theory, if we may indeed call it a theory and not an admonition. This may account for the fact that the reaction among Catholics and Protestants, exegetes and theologians, has ranged from unqualified enthusiasm to the suggestion of Modalistic Adoptionism. However, the *Choisir* article has removed some, at least, of the misunderstanding.

Secondly, there are certain questions which the dogmatic theologian must put to the Scripture scholar regarding the historical and philological foundations of Cullmann's idea:

a) To what degree is the entire New Testament the work of a distinctively Semitic, as opposed to a Hellenic, mentality? Especially as regards the fourth Gospel, granted that the Qumran discoveries have strengthened the case for the interpretation of John as reflecting a primitive Palestinian milieu, must this case be accepted as decisively established or merely as more probable in the present state of the evidence? Would such a respectable interpreter of the Fourth Gospel as C. H. Dodd, who interprets some of the key Christological passages in anything but a Semitic sense, still have solid backing among exegetes?

b) In interpreting the Christology of the New Testament, have Cullmann and others paid so much attention to the Semitic background of the authors as to neglect the Hellenic background of a large part of the audience? Have they paid sufficient attention, for example, to the fact that Paul is an apostle to the Gentiles and that he must make Christ intelligible to men of the Hellenic cast of mind? Dom Gregory Dix would seem to have paid more attention to this principle of interpretation than has Cullmann.

c) In New Testament times had there not already taken place between Jew and Greek such a mutual influence, for example through the Septuagint version of the Old Testament upon which the New Testament authors were heavily dependent and through which they read the Old Testament, that it would be something of a distortion to conceive of a Semitic functional mentality completely untouched by the Greek genius for inquiring into the being of things?

These are some of the questions which we must put to the Scripture scholars. They come down to this, perhaps: Now that the ghost of the Hellenization of Christianity by St. Paul has been laid and the links of the entire New Testament with the tradition of Israel given their due place, is it not time to stress what Jew and Greek had in common rather than what was peculiar to each? It is not likely that the answer to these questions will show that the problem raised by Cullmann is a completely false one; but perhaps it will help us to place the problem in a still more qualified and accurate way.

When this is done, then the dogmatic theologian, who is concerned with relating the sources of revelation among themselves, will have to put to himself some questions regarding the relationship of Chalcedon and the New Testament. Here are a few observations on this task:

a) While the further investigation of the New Testament may disclose that it is not absolutely or exclusively functional, there is certainly a relative functionalism which must be reckoned with. For example, certain texts tell us that Christ became *Kyrios* at the moment of His exaltation to the right hand of the Father. Supposing that these texts are speaking of a divine status, it would be heretical to take them ontologically and not functionally; they would in effect by affirming that He became God. Similarly, in seeking scriptural confirmation for the dogma of Chalcedon, the theologian must not too readily exclude the exegetical possibility that *morphe theou* and *morphe doulou* in the celebrated Philippians passage (2:6-7) refer not to nature but to function.

b) The legitimacy of Chalcedon in general, and of a Chalcedonian interpretation of the classic Christological texts in particular, is not established when one shows merely that the New Testament contains a hint or suggestion of its Chalcedonian equivalent, or that the latter is a natural and homogeneous prolongation of the former. It must be shown that the basic content of Chalcedon's affirmation is truly affirmed in Scripture, even though the expression of the affirmation may be quite different. *In eodem dogmate, eodem sensu eademque sententia,* said the Vatican Council (DB 1800) after Vincent of Lerins.

c) In this process of relating the two Christologies, more than a merely logical analysis of classic texts is required. The New Testament doctrine of the one and the many in Christ—and there is such a doctrine—must be examined in its proper characteristics.[19] Then this doctrine must be seen as the crown of a long preparation in the Old Testament, in which two general presentations of eschatological deliverance may be distinguished. God Himself will come to save His people and at the same time a man will be raised up as the herald and instrument of this salvation. It is only in the New Testament, in the reality of the God-man, that the convergence of these two lines (each of which has various modalities in the Old Testament) is perfectly achieved. Christ is both the preexistent Word of God who has come down, and the Prophet who has been raised up.

Thus Scripture already presents us with "ascending" and "descending" Christologies, though the expression is not identical with that of the Christologies of Antioch and Alexandria, respectively.[20]

d) Finally, if the theologian is to exploit to the full the resources of Scripture without doing violence to the rules of sound exegesis, he will have to approach his task with a realization that, while he must begin with critical exegesis, he must also go beyond it. He will have to call upon such key notions as that of the nature of revelation, the analogy of faith, the development of dogma, and perhaps most important of all, some theory of the senses of Scripture.

I know of no one who has undertaken the large task of thus integrally relating the Chalcedonian one-and-many to the scriptural one-and-many, using recent advances in biblical exegesis and theology, including whatever is acceptable in functionalism, using the methods of Grillmeier and Daniélou, relying on the basic notions of dogmatic development, the nature of revelation and the senses of Scripture, as tools. Till this is done, we should be grateful, I think, to the exponents of functionalism for the stimulus to doing it they have provided.

III

Even from what we have seen so far, it may be clear that Christology today is not merely repeating well worn formulas or holding the line against critics, but that attempts are being made to move forward our understanding of Christ. Perhaps this forward-moving character of current Christology can best be suggested by enumerating and briefly describing some particular proposals.

First of all, Father Karl Rahner, who in a notable essay has called for a spirit of enterprise in Christology,[21] advances in another article a threefold proposal in meditating on the basic formula: The Word of God became man.[22]

The *Word* became man—not the Father or the Holy Spirit. *Could* the Father or the Holy Spirit become man? Father Rahner, and with him Father Grillmeier, protest against our too ready acceptance, especially out of reverence for St. Thomas, of the idea that any one or two or all three of the divine persons could assume one or several human natures, singly or together.[23] They suggest that we look again at a stream of early patristic thought according to which the Father, by His personal character, could express Himself visibly and perfectly *ad extra* only through the Son, whose personal character it is to be the perfect expression of the Father within the Godhead, and, should God freely chose to create, to be the perfect expression of the Father *ad extra*. So far as I know, this proposal has remained general, and no one has attempted to argue for it in detail.

The Word became *man*. What is man? We may think, says Father Rahner, that we know what man is, that we can define him as rational animal quite independently of Christ; and our understanding of the Incarnation, which involves a true humanity, is contingent upon our understanding of man. But until we see man in Christ, until we realize that the openness of human nature involves a radical though obediential capacity for hypostatic union, a capacity which has been actuated only in one man but which is present in all men—until we do this, have we really understood the mystery that is man? Can it be that our understanding of man is contingent upon our understanding of the Incarnation? And that there is no adequate anthro-

pology that is not rooted in Christology? Rahner's preoccupation here would seem to be somewhat similar to that
of Karl Barth, even though the doctrinal presuppositions
would undoubtedly be different. Rahner develops this suggestion somewhat by showing that the meaning of human
nature is "to be the castaway, the abandoned, that which
perfects itself and reaches its true stature by continually
yielding itself to the Incomprehensible. But this occurs most
fully, to an unsurpassable degree, in the most radical form
possible, if this nature so abandons itself to the mystery
of fullness, is so emptied out that it becomes God's own."[24]
He also suggests the possibility of what he calls a transcendental deduction of the credibility of Christ which
would set out from the dual character of man, who is at
once a corporeal, concrete, historic being of earth, and a
being of absolute transcendence, and which would aim to
show that Christ is the objective correlative of this dual
structure of man.

The Word *became* man. What happens to the Word
when He *becomes* that which He was not before? The
Church tells us against Monophysism, that He does not
cease to be what He was, He is not transmuted, for He is
immutable. Scholastic theology, working from Aristotelian
metaphysics, tells us further that the Word does not even
acquire a new relationship; the Incarnation involves a real
relationship of the humanity to the Word, but not of the
Word to the humanity. We are justified in saying that
the Word became man, that the Word is man, because of
this unique new relationship of the humanity to the Word.
But nothing has happened within the Word; the Incarnation is not a new divine experience, but a human experience

had by a divine person. A new relationship in the Word would be an increase in perfection which is excluded by the divine immutability. Now neither Father Rahner nor Father Gutwenger are satisfied with this classic conception; they feel, that, among other things, it appears to evacuate the divine *kenosis* of any real content, to reduce the *factum est* to a manner of speaking. Gutwenger's proposal is to speak of a transcendental or structural real relation of God to the world by virtue of the decree of creation (hence also of the Incarnation), a relation identical with the divine essence, hence not violating the divine simplicity, a relation which in its *esse ad*, like the Trinitarian relations, says neither perfection nor imperfection, hence not violating the divine immutability and infinite perfection, and yet a real relation of God to the actual world, which means a certain modification in God without detriment to His immutability.[25] Rahner's proposal, I must confess, escapes my comprehension. His formula is that the Word, who is unchangeable in Himself, is changeable in another. I simply do not understand how this formula says anything which is both true and new. On the other hand, Rahner offers in the course of his argumentation an analogy which could well prove fruitful for our understanding of the Incarnation. Just as our affirmation of trinity in God does not compromise our affirmation of His absolute unity, and just as the concept of divine unity to which we naturally come cannot tell us directly what the trinity might be, so the affirmation of a certain modification in God by the Incarnation need not, he suggests, compromise our affirmation of that immutability which is required by the divine perfection. The analogy, I say, may be a fruitful one, but it hardly seems that we have the fruit as yet. Whereas St. Augustine's employment of the metaphysics of relation helped to a real *intelligentia fidei* regarding the divine trinity and unity, it is not yet clear that we have here such a positive insight into the compatibility of a real *factum est* with the divine immutability. In any case, this is one line of current effort at a better understanding of the Incarnation.

A final group of current studies is concerned with the enduring mediational and instrumental role of the humanity of Christ in our salvation. Here a whole series of questions, most of them traditional, are being examined, and there is a general convergence of answers toward a unified theory. The recent interest in the symbolic aspect of the sacraments, together with the realization of how much symbolism, especially of a liturgical provenance, is present in the Gospels, has led to the conviction that there is a wealth of material awaiting theological exploitation.[26] Both as regards the miracles of Christ in general and as regards the resurrection in particular, there has been a shift from emphasis on the physical and apologetic aspects to emphasis on the symbolic and kerygmatic aspects. The miracles of Christ, especially the resurrection, are signs of the presence of divine grace, the presence of God powerfully acting to bring salvation to His people according to a consistent pattern.[27] Karl Rahner has pointed out how theology in recent centuries has neglected the mysteries of the life of Christ prior to His passion; what possibilities are offered in the Gospel accounts of His baptism, temptation, transfiguration, for example, for a more complete speculative Christology. Especially if one favors a Caselian-type view of the presence of the mysteries of the life of Christ in the liturgical mysteries, or at least sees in the mysteries of His life in their very historical occurrence salvific causality not only by way of merit and satisfaction but, to use St. Thomas' phrase, *per modum cuiusdam efficaciae*, the way is prepared for a more adequate explanation of how the grace of Christ, head of His Body which is the Church, comes to His members. There is the further effort, suggested by Karl Rahner, and admirably executed by Juan Alfaro, to show how, notwithstanding the immediate character of the beatific vision, it is, from another point of view, essentially mediated by the humanity of Christ. In summary, the key notions of *sacramentum, instrumentum* and *ordo* are capable of yielding a Christology more perfectly structured in itself, better integrated with the theology of grace, the sacraments, the Church and the last things, and kerygmatically more satisfying.

If one had to sum up the principal efforts and opportunities in current Christology, it might be done in the following terms: First, an effort at integration, an attempt to integrate the conciliar with the scriptural, the ontological and objective with the psychological, subjective and personal, the sphere of being with the sphere of function, the strictly Christological with the soteriological, ecclesiological, sacramental and eschatological. Secondly, an effort at balance, on every level, between the legitimate exigencies of Alexandria and Antioch, the descending and ascending Christologies. Thirdly, an effort at translation, at showing the relevance of the theology of the God-man to modern man's life, and especially at finding in the mystery of the Incarnation the solid basis of that integral Incarnationalism that Christians are seeking today.[28]

NOTES

1. For general bibliography see A. Grillmeier and H. Bacht (editors), *Das Konzil von Chalkedon*, 3 volumes (Würzburg, 1951-1954), Vol. 3, pp. 825-865, as well as the footnote references in all three volumes. Also B. Xiberta, *Tractatus de Verbo Incarnato* (Madrid, 1954), Vol. 2, pp. 669-739.

2. K. Adam, *The Son of God* (New York, 1940), p. 1.

3. For the foregoing and following see the excellent essay by A. Grill-meier, S.J., "Die theologische und sprachliche Vorbereitung der christologischen Formel von Chalkedon," *Das Konzil von Chalke-don* (see note 1), volume 1, pp. 5-202. In English, J. N. D. Kelly, *Early Christian Doctrines* (2nd ed., London, 1960), Chs. 11 and 12, offers a fine summary of the Alexandrian-Antiochene dispute.

4. F. Sullivan, S.J., *The Christology of Theodore of Mopsuestia* (Rome, 1956).

5. J. McKenzie, S.J., "Annotations on the Christology of Theodore of Mopsuestia," *Theological Studies*, 19 (1958), 345-373; see also the reply of Fr. Sullivan, *ibid.*, 20 (1959), 264-279.

6. J. H. Newman, "An Essay on the Development of Christian Doctrine" (6th ed.; London, 1888), p. 343.

7. H. Diepen, *La théologie d'Emmanuel* (Bruges, 1960) is the most recent contribution to this discussion, and contains references to the principal articles of the author and other writers. Maritain's new position is presented by him in an essay, "On the Notion of Subsistence," in *Progress in Philosophy* (ed. J. McWilliams; Bruce, 1955), pp. 29-46; the same essay, together with his former position, is reprinted in the new edition of his *Distinguish to Unite, or, The Degrees of Knowledge* (New York, 1959), pp. 421-444.

8. P. Galtier, *L'unité du Christ* (Rome, 1939), pp. 237-371. For a good survey of the following discussion see J. Sweeney, S.J., "Some Recent Developments in Dogmatic Theology," *Theological Studies*, 17, (1956), 388-397.

9. B. Xiberta, *El Yo de Jesucristo* (Barcelona, 1954).

10. Cf. P. de la Trinité, "A propos de la conscience du Christ; un faux problème théologique," *Ephemerides Carmeliticae*, 11 (1960), 3-52.

11. On the ideas expressed in this paragraph see K. Rahner, "Chalkedon

—Ende oder Anfang," in *Das Konzil von Chalkedon* (see note 1), Vol. 3, pp. 20-25 (This provocative essay has been reprinted in Rahner's *Schriften zur Theologie* (2nd ed., Einsiedeln, 1956), Vol. 1, pp. 169-222, and translated into English in K. Rahner, *Theological Investigations*, Vol. I (London and Baltimore, 1961), 149-200; E. Gutwenger, *Bewusstsein und Wissen Christi* (Innsbruck 1960), pp. 143-149; J. Alfaro, "Cristo Glorioso, Revelador del Padre," *Gregorianum*, 39 (1958), pp. 244-247.

12. An extreme example of this tendency is the following statement: "Christus secundum habitum fuit non solum optimus dialecticus, philosophus, mathematicus, medicus, ethicus, seu politicus; sed etiam musicus, grammaticus, puta, rhetoricus, faber, agricola, pictor, nauclerus, miles, et sic de aliis," Salmanticenses, *Cursus Theologicus, Tractatus XXI: De Incarnatione*, disputatio XXII, dubium II, n. 29.

13. For recent discussions along these lines see the book of Gutwenger mentioned in note 11, and R. Haubst, "Die Gottanschauung und das natürliche Erkenntniswachstum Christi," "*Theologische Quartalschrift*, 137 (1957), 385-412; similar proposals were made over a decade ago by A. Durand, "La science du Christ," *Nouvelle Revue Théologique*, 71 (1949), 497-503.

14. Philadelphia, 1959. See the analytical review article of D. Stanley, S.J., in *Theological Studies*, 20 (1959), 409-421.

15. O. Cullman, *Choisir*, 1 (1960), 20-23. A survey of some critical reactions to the book may be consulted in *New Testament Abstracts*, 3, (1958-1959), 308-311. Worthy of special mention is the theological critique of L. Malevez, "Nouveau testament et théologie fonctionelle," *Recherches de Science Religieuse*, 48 (1960), 258-290.

16. G. Dix, *Jew and Greek A Study in the Primitive Church* (Westminster, 1953).

17. *Christology of the New Testament*, pp. 4, 326 f.

18. O. Cullmann, *Earliest Christian Confessions* (London, 1949).

19. This has been well done by A. Grillmeier in the essay mentioned in n. 3, *supra*, pp. 9-31.

20. For a development of the outline just given, see J. Daniélou, *The Lord of History* (Chicago, 1958), pp. 183-213; this is not merely a study in biblical theology, but an answer to the charge of anti-historicism leveled against Chalcedon. Add the same author's recent *Christ and Us* (New York, 1961), pp. 79-93.

21. See n. 11, *supra*.

22. K. Rahner, "Zur Theologie der Menschwerdung," *Catholica*, 12 (1958), 1-16; the article has appeared in French as "Réflexions

théologiques sur l'Incarnation," "*Sciences Ecclésiastiques,* 12 (1960), 5-19.

23. A. Grillmeier, art. "Christologie," *Lexikon für Theologie und Kirche,* Vol. 2, col. 1160.

24. K. Rahner, *Catholica,* 12 (1958), p. 5.

25. E. Gutwenger, *op. cit.,* pp. 114-121.

26. Cf. M. O'Connell, S.J., "The Sacraments in Theology Today," *Thought,* 36 (1961), 40-58.

27. Cf. L. Monden, *Le miracle, signe du salut* (Bruges, 1960); F. Durrwell, *The Resurrection* (New York, 1960).

28. For an excellent survey of current trends in Christology, see A. Grillmeier, "Zum Christusbild der Heutigen Katholischen Theologie," in J. Feiner *et al.* (eds.), *Fragen der Theologie Heute* (Einsiedeln, 1957), pp. 265-299; also the same author's contributions to the articles "Christologie" and "Jesus Christ" in the new edition of *Lexikon für Theologie und Kirche.*

Quentin Quesnell

>>>>><<<<<

MARY IS THE CHURCH

THE statement of Otto Semmelroth in his *Urbild der Kirche*,[1] one of the earliest of modern full-length treatments of the Mary-Church theme, is just as true today as when it was written ten years ago: "After inspecting the Church's tradition, one can no longer doubt the truth of the proposition: Mary is the prototype of the Church. We now have to try to bring this truth into proper relation and order with all the rest of the mysteries of Mary." One can certainly agree wholeheartedly with these words, no matter what reservations he feels obliged to make about

59

Semmelroth's later conclusion on the Mary-Church analogy ("typology" for him) as the fundamental principle of Mariology.

If indeed in 1950 one could no longer doubt about the truth of this analogy, what is to be said today? For our insights into the treasures of tradition have continued to multiply, and the facts to be collected. Especially has Scripture itself been revealing its secrets, so that what were a few years ago merely shrewd guesses as to Mary-Church in the gospel of John and in the Apocalypse have become practical certitudes.[2] In addition there is the growth of a strong probability that the same will soon be true of Luke's Gospel-Acts composite work and perhaps even of St. Paul's epistles.[3]

Let us begin this discussion, therefore, from the supposition that the facts are known. Let us take as commonly granted by scholars that there is an analogy between Mary and the Church, and that this analogy is presented in the sources of theology—Scripture, the Fathers, liturgy, the theologians.

Moreover, without implying that there is not very important work still remaining to be done along the line of positive investigation, let us also agree that enough facts are already on hand and enough certitude about their significance to make it imperative for us to move on to that second step: "We now have to try to bring this truth into proper relation and order with all the rest of the mysteries of Mary." The time has come for theological ordering, synthesis, and above all for understanding.

But true theological understanding can result only from asking true theological questions. And, if theology is a search for understanding, the most important theological questions must always begin with a "Why?" The central problems of theology are searches after causes—as steps to *the* Cause.[4] For the object of theology is traditionally God and all other things insofar as they are related to God. Faith guides the search, both by presenting some of the facts to be investigated and especially by determining the point of view from which those facts are to be considered. Hence this inquiry into the "why" of things must be carried out in the light of God's revelation, His manifest, official and public dealing with man in history, transcending history.

We can proceed, in regard to the Mary-Church analogy, to make such an inquiry. For, whether this analogy is a revealed truth or not (and the mere fact of its frequent occurrence in the sources does not really prove that it is), still, no one would deny that a full analysis of the causality behind the Mary-Church analogy will require or be considerably helped by the light of divine revelation.

Let this then be our chief question: Why the Mary-Church analogy? Why, in the light of divine revelation, is this analogy true and well grounded in the real world?

At once we are confronted with the necessity for a preliminary question, perhaps only materially theological, demanding a summing up of the results of previous positive researches: "Precisely what *is* this Mary-Church analogy? What do we mean by it? In what propositions can it best be summarily expressed?" It is about these propositions, then, that we shall ask later, "In the light of God revealing Himself and His plans, why are these things true?"

There will also be a consequent question of considerable importance: "What is the place of this truth in Mariology?

What implications has it for all the other truths in the field? And what, if anything, does it show about the place of Mariology in theology as a whole?"

These, then, are the three questions we must try to answer: Granting that there is a Mary-Church analogy in tradition and in Scripture, what precisely is this analogy? Why, in the light of divine faith, is it true? What further light does it shed on the rest of theological truth?

As to the first question: exactly what propositions are we to understand to be contained in the somewhat loose expression: "The Mary-Church analogy?" Positive research has already discovered several, and further research, coupled with reflective analysis will perhaps discover many more. Still, all those in use at present, all the things which a theologian is likely directly to "mean" when he speaks of "the Mary-Church analogy," seem reducible to at least one of the following five more or less classic formulations:[5]

1. Mary is the Church.

2. Mary and the Church share the same attributes (Mary is the Mother of Christ, the Church is the Mother of Christ; Mary is a virgin, the Church is a virgin, and so forth).

3. Mary is the prototype of the Church.[6]

4. Mary and the Church imply and demand one another, even in their respective, historical reality (i.e., the mediated, incarnational nature of the Christian religion is such that it must have a visible, hierarchical Church; and that Church, in which man, under grace, cooperates with grace, needs Mary the coredeeming Virgin Mother of God).[7]

5. Mary is the chief member of the Church.

Our investigation will be made still easier if we can put these five propositions into some clear order among themselves, reducing them still further. Therefore, let proposition 1, "Mary is the Church," be taken as the basic thesis. Actually there are many reasons, too long to be detailed here, why, on historical, scriptural and patristic, as well as merely logical grounds, this proposition would be looked upon as most basic among the five.

Proposition 2, "Mary and the Church share the same attributes," can be taken simply as defining the meaning of the basic thesis. That is, Mary is the Church in the sense that she and the Church share the same attributes, that what is predicated of the one may be and must be predicated of the other.

The third proposition, consequently, "Mary is the prototype of the Church," will be seen as an obvious conclusion of the basic thesis, Proposition 1, as defined by Proposition 2. For, if Mary and the Church share the same attributes, and if Mary, as a figure in history and in public revelation, preceded the Church, it follows that she was a prototype of the Church.

That Mary and the Church imply and demand one another in the sense explained is a secondary, though direct, consequence of the basic thesis. It is secondary inasmuch as it also presupposes the "prototype" proposition.

Finally, that "Mary is the chief member of the Church," whether we consider the Church as sanctifying or sanctified, redeeming or redeemed, is the partial reason why the basic thesis is true. Because it is a reason, though only partial, it comes, of course, under the heading of explanation, and will be treated more properly and at greater length later.

But before going on to our causal analysis, we could perhaps specify more precisely our analogy and our basic proposition. Thus we shall study the statement "Mary is the Church" in the sense that "Mary and the Church share the same attributes." And we shall try to discover why this proposition is true, taking it for granted that it has been a part of Catholic tradition.

But is the proposition really true? Granted that it is found in many of the Fathers and theologians, is it meant to be stated thus without limits? After all, most people would hardly admit that Mary has absolutely every attribute of the Church. She does not have over four hundred million members; she is not intrinsically and essentially hierarchical, with the Pope at Rome as her visible head; and she is not a visible society, founded by Christ.

Therefore there are limits. Yet, at the same time, we all know that Mary is the New Eve—with the Church; that she is Mother of men and Mother of Christ—with the Church; that she is the perfect virgin, most faithful bride, and spouse of the Lord of the Church, the one ark of salvation, the great sacrament, and so on, all with and in substantially the same way as the Church.[8]

By what criterion, then, do we spontaneously select various predicates for the two to share in common, and just as surely reject others? If we can express that criterion, we will have the inherent limit which we seek.

Let us suggest for the present that the criterion might be expressed as follows: whenever we consider the Church directly and formally in her salvific being and destiny, we find that her attributes are properly applicable to the Blessed Virgin considered in the same way. Consider the two from any other point of view, and the attributes cannot be transferred, or can be applied only in metaphor.

To put it another way: whenever we consider the Church precisely insofar as she brings God to man and man to God, whether we picture her as standing between man and God, distinct from both, or as partially identified with either of the two terms, we find that the Church can rightly be hailed in the same expressions as Mary similarly considered. The reason for this, and especially the interesting reason why we do not ordinarily advert explicity to this criterion though we use it so often, will be considered later.

We have just implied that the Mary-Church analogy, in the sense in which we are taking it, is not merely a metaphor. This too needs some explanation. Why is it not a metaphor?

A metaphor is not just any predication that identifies two substances or substantial natures not physically and simply one in reality. A metaphor is not even just "a simile, with the words 'like' or 'as' left out." A metaphor, in the exact sense in which we wish to use it here, is a distinct kind of predication with philosophically significant properties of its own. It is the predication of one nature of another, made because the subject possesses, in a manner exceeding his own proper nature, attributes looked on as characteristic rather of the nature of the predicate.[9] Thus I say John is a lion because John has, in a manner exceeding what I would expect of human nature, certain attributes which are looked on as characteristic of the nature of a lion.

It follows that a true metaphor is irreversible. One cannot say "This lion is a John" without a complete overturning of meanings. Nor is the difficulty here in the fact that one would be predicating an individual, for it is possible to say "This man is a Caesar." The substance named in the predicate must always be something immediately recognizable as characterized naturally and normally by some quality, some attribute, which the subject substance is here and now grasped as possessing in a marked and extraordinary way, over and above what we would expect of the limits of the subject's own nature.

Thus, if we say "The Church is Christ" or "Mary is Christ," we have the proper structural elements for metaphor. For the Church and Mary, and anything else which is not physically and actually the eternal Son of God become Man, can nevertheless be called Christ if it possesses in an extraordinary manner those attributes which are commonly recognized as characteristic of Christ. And, when we predicate in this way of the Church or of Mary, our predication is irreversible. We cannot say that Christ is the Church or that Christ is Mary except by shifting the meaning of the name Christ so as to form a new metaphor, or, by appealing to the mystical Christ, a real identity. The Church is the mystical Christ by identity. She is the historical Christ of Nazareth by metaphor.

Now the classical formulation of the Mary-Church analogy is not a metaphor in this sense. For Mary is the Church and the Church is Mary. The formula is completely reversible. We do not say Mary is the Church because Mary possesses, in a way disproportionate to her own nature, certain characteristics which the Church is well known as possessing naturally. Nor, when we say "The Church is Mary," meaning the historical Church and the historical Mary, is this because we recognize the Church as an extraordinary sharer in some quality which belongs by nature to Mary alone.

Rather, the truth is that from the point of view of their salvific significance both Mary and the Church share in an attribute which is, strictly speaking, proper to neither. This attribute, actually unnamed, by which one possesses the perfection of the saving God and the perfectibility of man who is saved, belongs by nature to One alone, the perfect Mediator, Jesus Christ. Mary and the Church are the two outstanding sharers in that attribute. But it remains a property which of itself can belong naturally to nothing merely created, and therefore to neither Mary nor the Church.

Still, this is not the whole story either. For if it were, it would follow that Mary and the Church are "like" each other. If John is a lion, because of courage, and Joseph is a lion, because of courage, then, in respect to courage, Joseph is like John.

Now Mary and the Church are each Christ because they share His saving power and perfect sanctity. But we do not say that they are "like" each other; we say Mary *is* the Church, and vice versa. This we cannot say of Joseph and John.

There are two reasons for this difference. First, both Mary and the Church are not just any two possessors of the "Christ attribute," the "salvation form." They are two outstanding possessors of it, indeed *the* two outstanding possessors. Each is singular in her excess of possession of the participated Christ form. Each is, next to Christ and in a way which does not require that we subordinate either to the other, supremely sanctifying and sanctified, saving and saved.

Secondly, that special aspect under which they have everything in common happens to coincide with the special aspect under which theology and the theologian, and revelation itself as revelation, always approach and consider them. That is, the aspect of their standing between man and God, what we have called their "salvific" aspect, their function in the dealings of God with man and the progress of man toward God, happens to correspond with the aspect under which theology, faith and revelation always look at their objects.

Thus, while it is of course not true that from all possible points of view Mary is the Church, nevertheless it is true from the one point of view which theology as theology always must take, and from the point of view of revelation taken formally as revelation. For theology and revelation always look on and present their objects under the aspect of their order to God as Principle and End of all things, primarily of man, and of all else through man. And this is, as a matter of fact, the order of salvation. This is to consider things in the light of their salvific significance.[10]

To an outsider, to a mere historian, for example, it would be enough, looking at the facts scholars have assembled, to say: Mary is like the Church under certain aspects just as Joseph is like John under the aspect of courage. But to the theologian, functioning formally as such, Mary will be like the Church each time he looks at her, and the Church will be just as much like Mary. All attributes predicable of the one, theologically speaking, will apply to the other. And this is conveniently and rightly summed up, and not by metaphor either, in the expression "Mary is the Church."

It is very much the same as the case of the chemist who

so annoys us by repeatedly refining man as "a compound of x and y and z." We say: "Ridiculous! He is ignoring the most important facts about man. Of course he will never discover a soul by chemical processes and techniques; but that does not mean that man is only a compound of x and y and z." Still, it remains true that, for the chemist, a compound of x and y and z would have such and such properties. And no matter how much he investigates a man, he always finds precisely those same properties. His necessary and correct conclusions, as a chemist, are "Man is a compound of x and y and z" and "Such and such a compound of x and y and z is a man."

So it is in the case at hand. Mary lived on a certain street in Nazareth. This is a fact, eternally true. But that it was this street and not some other has no salvific value that we know of as yet, and hence, probably, was never revealed. And if historians do or do not discover it, it is not likely to make much difference to a theologian as a theologian. Consequently we do not say that the Church lived or lives or will live on such and such a street in Nazareth.

But Mary was a daughter of Abraham and of David, a fact not merely related in the course of the Scripture story but formally revealed. It is the sacred author's clear intention to convey this as part of his message. Hence it is God's. And so the Church is and must forever be a daughter of Sion. Although we do not yet understand completely the real place of this truth in God's plan, our theology of the Old Law is still so little developed, we at least know and believe that the Jews are God's Chosen People, and that our salvation depends on our becoming children of Abraham too and our Church being the new Israel.

Now we are ready to ask our question "why?" The most direct answer to any "why" is a formal cause.[11] Why is a man a man? Because he has a soul, the form of a man. We have already indicated that behind the truth, "Mary is the Church," lies the mutual possession of a certain "form." Let us examine that form more closely.

What is this form which Mary and the Church have in common when considered in their salvific functions? It is not a "physical" form. They are not physically one, with a single act of existing. It is not the same "specific" form, as in man and man; though it more closely resembles this. Still it does not place Mary and the Church in any recognizable species.

The form they share in has no definite name, but its outlines are familiar enough. They are discernible wherever there is question of man's salvation, whenever one speaks of man's approach to God as End, and of relations with God as the sole adequate Helper and Mover toward Himself as End.

Nor is this form, which we called above the "Christ form," exactly what theologians mean by grace, though it might often approach that which less technical writings call grace. It includes grace, certainly, but it is itself clearly not a quality abiding in the substance of the soul. It includes something more than grace and it is not purely spiritual. Finally, it is not a share in God's own life, but only a means and a step thereto; and it perhaps includes intrinsically the awkwardnesses involved in transcending the limitations of one's own life and being in order to journey to God.

Perhaps "pattern" would be a better word than "form." For what we are describing is a pattern, a design, which a man's life and the events in it and somehow the man himself must assume if he is to be saved or to help save others. This pattern, judging from Scripture, has never changed since the first man sinned and mankind entered on an order of redemption. The elements which go to make it up have always included, on man's part, goodness, love of God, trials, trust in God alone for relief from trial, agony, death and apparent failure—all of which must be accepted lovingly and obediently at God's hands, in the firm belief and hope that, as He has willed and caused it all to happen, so He will make it come out all right in the end. The pattern culminates finally in resurrection or success out of failure, and resulting happiness, glory or eternal life.

These are the chief elements of the salvation pattern. Scholars point out how they are preached in roughly the same form in all the books of the Old Testament, and in all the figures, songs, parables and histories which go to make up that great collection.[12]

And Jewish students, who so long pored over the sacred page, found that same arrangement of the same elements in the overall design of the Sacred Books as a whole unfolding the story of their race; only for them the overall pattern is unfinished, the salvation lies still in the future. This pattern is the story of how God deals with fallen man, and of the dispositions and actions required of man if he is to go to God. By definitely assigned steps, and through trials, agonies, and deaths, he must move toward complete salvation, which will come about only from and through God.

This is how the Bible predicts a suffering and triumphing and God-among-us Messiah to come: by repeating over and over the outline structure of God's salvation. Thus all points forward to the One who, when He came, finally embodied all those elements at their highest and best in the one supreme exemplification of the God-man relationship, in the one perfect and complete Salvation.

Today any Christian can recognize that series of elements as a picture of the cross, of Christ's death and resurrection. Now that the great Sign has been given, the form once perfectly expressed in history, worked out in its fullness on the tortured and subsequently glorified body of God, all can recognize it in its lesser manifestations among lesser men. And everyone who would be saved himself or would lead others to salvation must participate in that form, feel it carved into his own life and being.

We can call this form, then, the salvation or redemption form or pattern; God's own appointed design for the life of man, fallen man, who wishes to attain God as End to be possessed. In a given moment of history, God spelled that pattern out for us as never before, in a way that would live and impress itself on the minds of all men for all ages to come, when He, having been made man, died on the cross for our salvation. We may call this form the form of the cross or perhaps of the Crucified. There is another and true sense, familiar to St. Paul, in which we can say simply that this form is Christ.

Many participate in this form, each in his own degree. The individual Christian is marked with it at baptism, and must try to grow into it more and more perfectly through his whole life. Those whom God loves most will wear it most. Those who are to have the most intimate part in the redemption of the world and to be themselves most perfectly redeemed, will also most outstandingly and visibly wear that same form.

Thus the Church presents that form to the world in an always marked and outstanding way. Always she is militant, suffering, triumphant, all at once. Always she is beset within and without, yet is always rejoicing; dying, behold! she is always living. Always she is moving toward God, away from the world, living in hope and trust and faith in Him who is always saving her out of every trial and always purifying her in new ones which she, as a body, is always bearing with Christ in perfect resignation and great love, praying for her enemies and giving thanks to God. And this love she always expresses in the act of most perfect sacrifice, sent up without cease from her altars around the world. She is the bride without spot or wrinkle, perfect, beloved, yet suffering always, even as He, the dearly beloved Son and Victim.

Consider St. Paul's frequent references to her. He lives in the age of the apostles, to whom Christ has "opened all the Scriptures"; and he lives under the special guidance of the Holy Spirit "who will teach you all things." Referring to the Church at Corinth, at Philippi, at Thessalonica, he exhorts the Christians, as individuals, like himself, and as groups to grow up together into the fullness of Christ according to the same pattern, keeping the commandments, love, endurance under trial, patience and long-suffering, faith and hope, thanksgiving; looking toward being glorified with Christ as they have suffered with Him, filling up His sufferings for His body which is the Church.[13]

This preaching of Paul's, and his use of the Old Testament to support it, serves as model for the typology of the

Fathers. From Paul's treatment of the Church as Christ, doing in her agony what Christ did, and what each apostle does, bringing forth Christ in Christians, the Fathers approached "ecclesiology"; and they saw eventually its connection with the physical and moral facts of the life of the Blessed Virgin and with her own salvific role.

She too was chosen, elected and preelected out of all mankind to be most after Christ what God wants man to be. She, most closely with Christ, brings about the salvation of men, and is herself, of all, most perfectly sanctified and redeemed. Mary then must bear the form in a supreme manner, manifested to the world. Sinless, loving and beloved, she too must learn to suffer, renounce, lean confidently upon the apparently afflicting arm of God and wait in confidence for her salvation. She bears this mark, these elements of salvation are found in her most perfectly: her perfect sinlessness from the first instant; her suffering coredemption with pierced soul; her unwavering faith; and her rewarding assumption and glory, being called blessed by all generations.

The partial cause of Mary's supreme participation in this form is that she is to be chief member of the Church. As chief member, she is to show most what the whole body aims at and will attain to, and would bring each of its members to. These things have happened to Mary historically. For the Church, many of them are still in the future. She is the chief member, toward whom the rest of us struggle in order to receive, as she has, Christ's pattern of salvation.

All who participate in this one form, no matter in what degree, can, from the salvific point of view, be symbols and types of one another. This will include individuals, groups, historical events, sacred signs and sacraments intended to convey the same message. This is why the index to Migne (Latin) can list seventy-four Old Testament figures for the Church and another fifty for the Blessed Virgin, besides another hundred names and comparisons.[14] None of these is as perfect and full to the point of identification as the two supreme instances, but every one of them does show forth the one form, each in its own way. The medieval tradition of reading so much of Scripture as applying first to Christ, then to Mary and the Church, and finally to the individual Christian soul, is amply justified.[15]

Scholastically speaking, then, the analogy of the Church and Mary has its formal cause in this redemption form, this salvation pattern, of death and resurrection, which may be summed up as the form of the cross, or simply as Christ. He is the one supreme exemplification or exemplar cause of everything else existing according to this pattern. Mary and the Church are the supreme participators of this form. They are, in Christ, what we shall be; Mary completely, the Church from day to day.

Still, this form does not ever belong to Mary or the Church perfectly as their own. They, like all other participators, depend for their possession entirely on Christ and His continuing influence. Therefore the efficient cause of the truth of this analogy is always God, acting through Christ's human nature as conjoined instrument. And it is also God working at the same time through, as secondary instruments, the very acts and being of the sanctified and sanctifying persons themselves. These persons present the matter to God; and the matter is their own acts and dispositions, thoughts and words and acts, bodies and souls, to be molded to the form of Christ. They present these, submitting and abandoning themselves to God the Spirit, Who thus and then inhabits, lives in them, working to accomplish this end.

This act of providing properly disposed material is a very important kind of instrumental cooperation, as for instance in the case of human parenthood. And, since it is indispensable, the man, the Church, in every age, must do what in them lies if the pattern is to be worked out and salvation attained. They must face each situation and master it by their own efforts, generously expended. But they must not trust in their own efforts for real success. For that they must look only to God. And when the pattern is complete, when darkness, suffering, and death have been successfully undergone and yielded finally to triumph, glory and life, then the credit for the successfully woven pattern must be placed wholly where it belongs—in God's hands.

The end of all this? Ultimately, the perfection and fullness of all things in their return to God. Proximately, Mary and the Church work to bring men to assimilate this pattern of salvation more clearly and easily and surely. The analogy itself has as its proximate end the praise of the glory of His grace; the pointing of minds and hearts alike to the Prime Analogate. This is done when both Mary and the Church are seen as showing forth that one supreme pattern which they both fall short of, while at the same time surpassing all other known instances of participation and imitation of it. "Be imitators of me, as I also am of Christ," they say with, and with greater right than St. Paul.

Our third question asked about the place of this analogy in Mariology, its relation to other Mariological truths, and what light, if any, it shed on the place of Mariology in the whole of theology.

Attention to the Mary-Church analogy has led us to attention to the salvation form. Now we cannot help but wonder if the whole of Mariology might not be seen as a study of the salvation form as embodied in Mary. The truths of her immaculate conception and lifetime of perfect virtue, coredemption, assumption and reign, would be only the spelling out in grand and unmistakable terms of the elements in the one great design, foretold by the prophets, living in Christ, and to be aimed at by every soul that hopes to save or be saved.

This same design might unify the study of the Church in an ecclesiology which was strictly theological and focused attention mainly on the Mystical Body, "than which no more noble, sublime, or divine" name for the Church can be found.[16] The image of the crucified and yet triumphing Christ would be traced in every single age and also seen as stretching over the centuries in one grand design, the necessity for which has been built into His body's human constitution.[17]

Perhaps every one of the standard tracts in theology might be viewed as a different approach to the one pattern of salvation, found now in Christ Himself, now in Mary or the Church, now in the sweep of all creation and the whole highly condensed history of angels and men. One tract might study its workings within the souls of men, from what dispositions it takes its rise, what affections it produces there, and by what great gifts. Another would analyze how it has its roots and its ultimate intelligibility in the triune reality of the one God who creates, redeems, and sanctifies as He does because of what, or rather who, He is.

Perhaps we can find here a tessera of true theological progress. Perhaps as long as we present and clarify doctrine that can be reduced to these basic elements we are on the right track. But if we wander off into teaching that lacks this salvific significance, although we may be doing spade-work for later theology, we may be merely lapsing into gnosticism. Recent studies in scriptural and "kerygmatic" theology would tend to confirm this.[18]

What of the fact that the norms under discussion seem to allow for a Josephology or a Joannolgy, or any other name-ology at all? Is not any man's life salvifically significant and reducible to these elements, how God has worked out the great Design in this one instance? True, but to make a theological study of such a man, we would have to work from inside him, or rather from inside God. For we would have to know exactly what the subject of our study experienced, how he reacted to how much grace in exactly what kind of temptations, and so on. This is the kind of knowledge and insight into human situations which will astound us at the last judgment when God's ways are finally justified to men. But at present we have such knowledge of other men only when God reveals it. So far as we understand revelation at present, we have not been given that knowledge about very many. We are grateful to know what we do about Mary.

NOTES

1. (Würzburg, 1950) p. 36.
2. Cf. F. M. Braun, *La Mère des fidèles* (Tournai-Paris, 1953); B. J. LeFrois, S.V.D., *The Woman Clothed with the Sun* (Rome, 1954); etc.

3. Cf. Jean Galot, S.J., *Marie dans l'Evangile* (Paris-Louvain, 1958); R. Laurentin, *Structure et théologie du Luc I-II* (Paris, 1957).

4. Cf. Bernard Lonergan, S.J., "The Concept of *Verbum* in the Writings of St. Thomas Aquinas," in *Theological Studies* 7 (1946), 359-372.

5. "Analogy" here includes only likenesses, not all possible relationships (e.g., "Mary Is the Mother of the Church").

6. For the importance of these first three propositions in the early Church, cf. especially Yves Congar, "Marie et l'Eglise dans la pensée patristique," in *Revue des Sciences Philosophiques et Théologiques*, 38 (1954), 3-38.

7. Karl Barth is frequently quoted in this connection: *Die Kirchliche Dogmatik*, I, 2 (1938), 157 and 160.

8. Cf. notes 6 and 14.

9. Cf. Robert R. Boyle, S.J., "The Nature of Metaphor," in *The Modern Schoolman* 31 (1954), 257-280.

10. For more on salvific significance and the following interpretation of the sacred author's intention, cf., e.g., Karl Rahner, "Le Principe Fondamental de la Théologie Mariale," in *Recherches de Science Religieuse* 42 (1954), esp. 481-483. Also "Nimm das Kind und seine Mutter," in *Geist und Leben* 30 (1957), 14-16.

11. Cf. Lonergan, *art. cit.*, 363-364; also in *Insight* (New York, 1957), 77-78.

12. Cf., for example, John L. McKenzie, *The Two-Edged Sword* (Milwaukee, 1956), 206-210; 237-245. Cf. also Congar, *art. cit.*, p. 17, note 32, and references there.

13. E.g., II Cor 5:7 ff; Phil 1:27-30; 3:8-21; I Thess 2:13-16; Col. 1:10 ff; etc.

14. PL 219, 672-674; also 247-250.

15. E.g., Denis the Carthusian, *Enarratio in Canticum Canticorum Salomonis*, where each chapter of the Canticle is systematically applied in sequence to Mary, Church, soul. *Opera Omnia*, 7 (Monstrolii, 1898), 289-447.

16. Pius XII, *Mystici Corporis* in *AAS* 35 (1943), 199.

17. Cf. Henri de Lubac, *Méditation sur l'Eglise* (Paris, 1953), 175-203 esp.

18. For example, Josef Jungmann, S.J., *Katechetik* (Wien, 1955), 291-315, and the references there.

Matthew J. O'Connell

>>>>><<<<<

THE SACRAMENTS IN
THEOLOGY TODAY

THE question: what does "sacrament" mean to a present-day theologian, is not an easy one to answer. The reason for this is not a lack of sound understanding. It is rather that "sacrament" has become, in recent decades, a very rich concept, too complex to be expressed, without danger of misunderstanding, in the once common definition: "an efficacious sign of grace." Partly responsible for this enriching of our understanding of the Christian sacraments is the "return to the Fathers." Our knowledge of how the sacraments have been understood through the centuries

80

has been greatly extended. We have, as a result, been able to regain or to revitalize fundamental insights formulated by the Fathers apropos especially of baptism and the Eucharist but valid for the whole sacramental economy.

It cannot be said, however, that present-day theologians have thus far done justice to these insights and principles or developed a satisfyingly structured view of sacrament as such and of the sacramental system. We are, as far as a speculative and systematic sacramental theology is concerned, still in a transitional period. The following pages, therefore, attempt simply to describe certain major orientations in contemporary systematic sacramental theology. They do not claim to present a complete picture of current theological thought nor even, in what is said, to speak for all theologians.[1]

The simplest way to understand and appreciate the contemporary development will be to begin by describing the emphases that were customary in the study of the sacraments from the time of the Council of Trent (closed in 1565) to the present century.

I

At the risk of oversimplifying and caricaturing the approach to the sacraments that was common in the centuries after Trent, we might describe it as follows. It was, first of all, centered on the dogmatic definitions of Trent. This means that the theological structure was being determined, willy-nilly, by polemic concerns. For it was Trent's explicit purpose to concentrate on a denial of Protestant errors. In the decree on sacramental principles (as also in the de-

crees on baptism and confirmation) this polemically
determined one-sidedness is more in evidence than elsewhere. The reason is that in this decree, unlike many others,
there is no discursive doctrinal synthesis prefixed to the
list of anathemas against specific errors. Such preliminary
doctrinal essays, even if they do not always aim at completeness, at least aided later theologians, when dealing with
sectors of theology that Trent had touched on, not to take
the polemic intentions of the Council as theological norms.

In any case, the general sacramental principles formulated
by Trent in a series of anathemas are presented simply as
an appendix to the conciliar decree on the justification of
sinful man by God. Thus there is little in Trent, apart from
passing remarks in the doctrinal essays on particular sacraments, to counteract the fragmentary and isolated character
of these anathemas. Owing precisely to their polemic purpose the anathemas have their axis in the notion of objective
sacramental efficacy. It was primarily this, as well as the
existence of any sacraments besides baptism and the Eucharist, that the Protestants were denying. They did not deny
the sign aspect of the sacraments. Consequently, Trent
alludes to this only in passing. The Tridentine emphasis on
efficacy (*ex opere operato*) was to be taken as normative
by theological treatises on sacramentality through the whole
post-Tridentine period, down almost to the last forty years.
The sacraments were, indeed, always said to be signs, but
this fundamental concept played no truly determinative role
in the theological scheme.

The results of this almost exclusive stress on efficacy, with
all else being regarded primarily as conditions of such
efficacy, were numerous. Many priests, and the few laymen

who might venture into the world of the theological manual, took away from this sector of theology the impression that Christian sacramentalism was in large measure a matter for the canon lawyer. Quantitative questions seemed to be primary; as a result, a certain casuistry, legitimate enough in its own sphere, crept in, and with it the air of arbitrariness and legalism that accompanies a casuistry cut off from its ontological principles. More concretely: in addition to objective efficacy, the determination of the exact "matter and form" (the ritual action and the accompanying, interpretative formula) became a central problem; validity became the primary focus of attention; infant baptism, despite disclaimers, became the model sacrament because it showed most clearly the objective character of sacramental efficacy, the independence of the sacraments from the inner attitudes of the recipient except as these were simply dispositions for grace. The long dispute on the kind of intention which the minister must have was largely carried on in this atmosphere. The treatise, with its fundamentally rather mechanistic viewpoint, was crowned by a discussion of the nature of sacramental causality in which the proper being of the sacraments as symbolic actions was left out of consideration.

A second result of the stress on efficacy was a double paradox in regard to the effect of the sacrament. The first was this: grace is effected by the sacrament, yet it was very difficult, once efficacy was isolated from the sign aspect of the sacrament, to grasp the intelligibility of specifically sacramental grace. This latter was usually said to consist of santicifying grace, or "common" grace: a basic grace that justifies and sanctifies man, and is everywhere and always absolutely the same, plus—what? Some theologians said the extra something was a right to further actual graces that would be needed to fulfill the obligations and attain the ends to which each sacrament committed one. This solution meant that the specifically new reality of sanctification was exclusively of the juridical order. It meant, further, that a right was being given to that to which every man already had a right, once he was baptized or otherwise justified. Other theologians proposed, to explain the extra something, various kinds of new supernatural habits; but each of these theories fell down before the fact that the purposes of any such habits were already to be attained by sanctifying grace itself and by the theological and moral virtues.

The second paradox was that attention was focused on the isolated individual, since he is properly and immediately the one sanctified, yet practically nothing was said of the role of this individual who in the sacramental action encounters God reconciling the world to Himself in Christ. All attention was necessarily turned, by reason of the starting point of the discussion, namely, the objective efficacy of the sacrament, to the denial of any contribution by the recipient and his merits to this efficacy. The recipient needs only be disposed—the very word "disposed" betrays the causal viewpoint, and shows that he is being considered simply as the passive recipient of the objectively efficacious sacrament. Beyond this, there was perhaps a brief word on the recipient's need of an intention as one of the conditions for the valid reception of a sacrament that somehow seemed to exist "out there"; and some notations on what his dispositions ought concretely to be.

The third large result of the Tridentine polemic stress on efficacy, when erected into the basic principle of a theological synthesis, was a certain number of omissions. In the treatise nothing was said of the role of the Church in the constitution of the sacraments; of the significance of the minister's intention which, once grasped, would not indeed have necessarily resolved the old dispute about what precisely he must intend to do but would have undercut this dispute and reduced it to its proper proportions; of the role of the recipient in the very constitution of the sacramental action. Nothing was said, either, of the sacraments as symbolic actions of Christ in His Church; as symbolic actions whereby the Church expresses what it is, namely the community of men who live in Christ (this chiefly in the sacramental sacrifice) and the effective visible continuation through time of the salvific will of God that was made definitively present in the world in the redemptive Incarnation; as symbolic actions, finally, whereby the Church also constitutes itself, ever renews itself through time as the hierarchically organized, socially structured community of those who answer the call to a supernatural destiny in Christ.

It is precisely on all these more or less neglected aspects of the Christian sacraments that several factors have, in the last two generations, focused theological attention and made possible the regaining of a fuller, more balanced view of the sacramental order. We have been in process of regaining and developing the patristic view of sacrament: specifically, the view of St. Augustine, which remained vital in Western theology until into the Middle Ages. In the thirteenth century we find the Augustinian insights being deepened and incorporated by St. Thomas in his *Summa* into an extraordinarily rich structure of sacramental principles. Among the factors in this recovery two stand out. The first is the liturgical movement which turned attention to three points. The very concern with the liturgy, recalling the theologian to the living source of data for theological reflection on the sacraments, brought home the fundamental fact that the sacraments are, first of all, symbolic actions. They are not things, nor actions in the abstract, but significative or symbolizing actions constituted here and now by the minister and the recipient in their distinct but complementary roles. The phrase "first of all" is used deliberately. For the efficacy of the sacraments is a strictly mysterious reality, and to get any understanding of it the theologian must look first to what is directly accessible to him, the human reality of symbolic action, which God has chosen to make the bearer of supernatural significance and efficacy.

The liturgical movement also highlighted the ecclesial dimension of the sacraments. The sacraments are ecclesial in a double sense. First, they are administered by the Church as her sacraments and, consequently, they give expression to what the Church is. Second, their immediate effect is to give to the individual recipient a series of "situations in the Church," as it were, wherein he is sanctified and whereby either the Church is given its juridico-hierarchic structure (baptism, orders) or certain fundamental mysteries and states of Christ are continued in His mystical Body.

The final point emphasized by the liturgical movement is that the ministerial sacramental actions of the Church are acts of cult in which Christ is the chief Priest, prolong-

ing the worship He began on earth, and in which He sanctifies men, applying to them the assimilative power of His
earthly mysteries.

The second major factor in the renewal of sacramental
theology has been a double insistence concerning grace, fos-
tered by the deepening of the theology of the mystical
Body. Our grace is the grace of Christ, in the sense that
Christ not only merited all grace in the present economy of
salvation, but is also the exemplar and the effective-instru-
mental cause of this grace through the mysteries of His
life, death and resurrection. Grace is, secondly, not a
thing: it is, on God's side, the gift of God communicating
Himself to man, and, on man's side, the transformation of
his person in response to the new presence of God, a transformation in which he is configured to Christ in whose grace
and whose response to God he now participates.

If we bring together these various threads and interests,
we might describe a Christian sacrament as a symbolic
action whereby Christ continues in and through His Church
the perfect cult of His earthly mysteries and whereby He
sanctifies His members, configuring them to Himself and
by that very fact dynamically ordering them to the fulfillment of salvation in the vision of God.

Even this incomplete description shows a sacrament to
be a many-sided reality. There is, however, a central concept which enables us to organize and synthesize all the
various aspects of a sacrament: the concept of symbolic
action. Here sacramental theology can benefit, and has
already begun to benefit, by the extensive interest in symbolism in other disciplines: in philosophical anthropology;
in experimental and depth psychology; in literary criticism.

About this central concept it seems possible to develop a synthesis of sacramental principles which would neglect nothing of what was canonized by Trent and developed during the post-Tridentine period, but would also take into account the insights gained or regained during recent decades.

II

Properly to understand the sacraments as symbolic actions which are cultic as well as sanctifying, and sanctifying because cultic, we need to see them as part of a larger "sacramental" order which is coextensive with the economy of salvation realized through Christ and the Church. The sacramental principle, the effective and operative presence of divine salvific reality under the veil of created symbols, is realized in three interrelated ways: in Christ the incarnate Word, in the Church as the mystical Body, and in the sacraments in the narrower sense of the word, that is, in symbolic ritual actions.[2]

First, in Christ the incarnate Word. Because of the hypostatic union with the Word, the humanity of Christ, as manifested and interpreted to us by its activity and by the word-revelation of Christ Himself, is the visible sign of God present in the world as Savior. It is, moreover, the effective sign. From the first moment of the Incarnation on, God is already beginning to sanctify the human race and has already committed Himself to the consummation of redemption through the passion, death and resurrection of the Son. The humanity of Christ is thus the visible and effective sign of the presence in the world of the salvific

will of God. We may express this same idea in another
way: the humanity of Christ is the sign of the new and
definitive covenant, effectively offered to humanity in the
person of God Himself, irrevocably united to a human
nature. Such an offering of covenant means, concretely,
God's invitation to, His demand for, love and fidelity from
the human race which Christ represents. By such love and
fidelity alone can mankind be saved. The response to this
gracious divine love is perfect on the part of Christ. All His
human actions, from the beginning of His incarnated existence, proceed in the spirit expressed in Hebrews 10:5-7:
The Son of God enters the world and says, "Behold, I come
to do Thy will, O God." Here is the response of love and
obedience, rendered to the Father by Christ who loves and
obeys not for Himself alone but in the name and person
of all men. These He draws to Himself in His all-embracing
knowledge and love, and assumes them into His own filial
relationship to the Father. In other words, Christ's humanity
and its activity are, to the eyes of faith, the visible and
effective symbol, the sacrament, of a double reality. They
are the sacrament of the descent of grace in the form of
reconciliation and covenant graciously offered by God.
They are the sacrament, too, of humanity's perfect worship,
of its complete and perfect union with God, mankind's
Creator, Lord and Blessedness, and of the ratification by
Christ, as Head of the race, of the covenant offered to
mankind.

In the divine plan it was the mysterious will of the Father
that reconciliation and redemption should be accomplished
through the blood of His Son. The sacrifice of the cross
is the necessary climax of Christ's mission. It is in this

moment, too, that Christ's humanity becomes most perfectly a visible and effective symbol, a sacrament. For his death and resurrection are the complete symbolic expression of both the movements already described, that is, of the descent of grace and of the redemptive response of Christ in worship.[3] It is the most eloquent revelation of the descent of grace, that is, of the divine salvific mercy, of the Father's will to save us, which is at the origin of our redemption: for on the cross God gave His own Son that no one might perish. It is, at the same time, the unsurpassable expression, namely, sacrifice, of Christ's worship and of His acceptance of the covenant: for He seals His loving obedience and ratifies the covenant in His own blood. Finally, and precisely because it is the act of perfect worship, of filial love and obedience, the sacrifice of the cross is the act most symbolic of, and effective of, our redemption.

The second realization of that sacramental principle which was established in the Incarnation as a fundamental principle of the Christian economy of salvation, is the Church.

The salvation of every man depends on his attaining union with the humanity of Christ the Saviour. This union is the work of faith and charity. But for those who with faith and love approached the mortal Christ on earth union with Him had a special dimension. For them, the encounter with the visible Christ was an encounter with God in person, with the invisible God through the medium of the visible humanity of God. And it was an effective encounter. Its efficacy indeed required the faith and love of those who came into contact with Christ, but it was nonetheless an efficacy mediated through the visible gestures and words of Christ, as He worked miracles, forgave sins, called men to discipleship. There was thus made possible for Christ's contemporaries a sacramental encounter in a very privileged sense of the word "sacrament." There was possible for them a salvific encounter with the invisible divine world, not only in and through the visible creation of God, but in and through visible creation assumed into the person of the Word of God Himself.

A similar encounter with God has been made possible for later generations through the Church. The Church, in H. de Lubac's phrase, is the sacrament of Christ, as Christ is the sacrament of God. There is indeed no hypostatic union between Christ and the Church as there is between humanity and divinity in Christ. But the same effective symbolic function that belongs to Christ's humanity by reason of the hypostatic union is shared in by the Church, by reason of the supramoral, ontological union that exists between Christ and the Church, His mystical Body and His Bride. It is in this sense that the Church is the prolongation of Christ and even, if we use the word in a limited and analogous sense, the "incarnation" of Christ. The Church, that is, is the visible and effective sign of the presence in the world of that divine salvific mercy which reconciled the world to Itself in Christ. The Church is the visible sign, in human history, of redemption accomplished, and the effective sign of its communication to men.

All this the Church is by its very being, as this is known by faith. To reach the individual, however, the Church must as it were actualize itself as the medium of salvation. This it does in all its proper activities, for these are all in one or other fashion, directly or indirectly, sanctifying.

But it is in the seven sacraments, the third and final realization of the sacramental principle, that the Church most fully actualizes itself as sanctifying. When this happens, the Church, formally as the sign and medium of salvation, encounters the individual, and in this encounter with the Church the individual encounters Christ, and God in Christ.

One facet of this sanctifying encounter of Church and man must not be overlooked. Just as Christ redeemed and sanctified the race in principle by His perfect cult, so the Church exercises her role as sanctifier precisely insofar as she exercises her cultic role. The seven sacramental rites are part of the Church's public worship, that is, the worship of the people of God, in union with Christ, the first though invisible Priest. The Church in her liturgy "sacramentalizes," that is, gives visible historical expression to, the cult of Christ, in a memorial of the "mysteries of His flesh," particularly of His death and resurrection. These mysteries are celebrated no less, though differently, in the sacraments and the divine office than in the sacramental sacrifice of the Eucharist. To put the matter briefly: in the sacraments, it is insofar as Christ in and through the Church renders symbolically and really present the love and obedience once rendered visible on the cross, that He brings the fruits of redemption to individual men through the ministry of the Church.

III

Against this background of the sacramental structure of redemption and the Church a theology of Christian sacramentality as embodied in the seven sacraments can be developed. In the sacraments we are concerned with social cultic acts of Christ, done in and through His Church. In and through these acts He applies the value and efficacy of His redemptive mysteries to the individual members of the Church. This means that the starting point for a theology of sacrament will be the nature of sacrament as a symbolic activity of the Church. The following paragraphs attempt simply to sketch, again without pretense at completeness, some broad lines along which a theology of sacrament is being developed; the complete treatise does not yet exist, and probably cannot yet be written at the present time.

SACRAMENTAL RELIGION

What is today often called "sacramental" religion, is not a uniquely Christian thing, but a universal phenomenon, founded in the religious and social psychology of man as an incarnate spirit living in a world with other men. Material things are for man the natural and spontaneous means of interpreting his religious experiences, not only to others but also, and first of all, to himself. He uses corporeal reality, including primarily his own corporeal self, to give symbolic expression to realities of a higher order. Instead of corporeal "reality," we ought properly and specifically to speak of corporeal human actions, in which objects distinct from man's own body may or may not be used. These actions are sign-actions, and they are the medium in which interior religious experience expresses itself and comes to full consciousness of itself. When this activity is social, it will almost inevitably be codified, and so we have "ritual" in the proper sense. Such codification is by no means an arbitrary thing, nor are ritual prescription and individual spontaneity to be simply opposed. Otherwise we could not account for the fact that certain symbolic gestures and the symbolic use of certain natural objects tend to be universal, either absolutely or at least within large cultural complexes. The universality of certain patterns of symbolic religious expressions has been brought home to us by the comparative history of religions, in the work, for example, of Mircéa Eliade. And we have learned how deeply rooted in man these symbolisms are, thanks to the psychological investigations of C. G. Jung and his school, where the data accumulated are of great value, independently of the validity of Jung's theories.

Such symbolic religious actions give expression to man's conception of God and of his relationship to Him. Ultimately they express man's desire for communion with whatever "god" he believes in; they voice a self-giving which is an active receptiveness, or, in our own traditional terms, they express man's sense of dependence on a supreme being, in its various aspects of adoration, thanksgiving, repentance, petition.

SIGNS OF ECCLESIAL FAITH

In the Christian sacraments, as indeed in all the liturgical activity of the Church, we are dealing with symbolic activities that give expression to the Church's religious faith. In them the Church attests, and exercises, its fundamental function of continuing the worship of God initiated by Christ. It attests, too, its knowledge that it depends entirely on God for that sanctification and salvation of its members at which its worship also aims. A liturgical act is a social

cultic act of petition by and for the Church; whatever be
its outward shape and verbal formula, a liturgical act is
always a profession of faith in God and a prayer for sanctification. In the Christian liturgy, "faith" is, of course, not
simply a belief founded in natural religious experience. It
is *fides ex auditu*, faith in response to the word of the
Self-revealing God, and what is prayed for with faith is a
supernatural sanctification, a transcendent union with God
in Christ.

What has so far been said of symbolic action and the role
of faith might be called the natural and Christian substruc-
ture of the Church's sacramental life in the narrower sense
of the word "sacrament," and it cannot be overlooked in
attempting to understand the seven sacraments.

SYMBOLS OF GRACE

When we concentrate on the seven sacraments as seven
privileged forms of Christian ecclesial symbolic activity,
an important note, specific to the seven sacraments, catches
our attention.

Any external gesture or verbal formula can be the expression of man's interior supernatural religious experiences
—a genuflection, a raising of his hands to God, any attitude
of prayer, any set of words. What is proper to the sacraments as symbolic actions is, first of all, that not only are
they a prayer, but they also symbolize that inner sanctification for which man prays. "The sacraments signify grace."
It would be better, in this classical formula, to speak of
"symbolizing" instead of "signifying." The word "sign"
has been debased and calls to mind the image of a signal of

some kind or at best of a printed placard or billboard. "Sign" thus understood cannot do justice to sacramental activity.

When it is said that "grace" is signified or symbolized, grace ought to be understood very concretely. Grace is often thought of in abstract fashion as a supernatural quality of the soul. Such a concept is, of course, valid, and quite necessary for certain purposes. But if one restricts oneself to it, it becomes once again impossible to do justice to the sacraments as symbolic action. Grace is the ontological transformation of the human person and his conformation to the divine being, due to the self-communication of God to the soul. But even this statement is not yet concrete enough. It is true, but it is true of grace in any possible supernatural order and is not yet specified as the "grace of Christ." In the present divine economy of salvation, grace is indeed the principle of the soul's transformation and its conformation to God. This transformation is, however, effected through the configuration of man to Christ in whom all the virtualities of created grace are present and all the modes of sanctity realized in formal or eminent fashion. In His fullness all others share; from Him all other grace derives.

What is proper to the Christian sacraments is therefore, first of all, that they symbolize the sanctification prayed for, which can now be expressed as the configuration of man to Christ. Secondly, they symbolize grace, not in a purely speculative, timeless way nor even simply as presenting the object of the Church's petition, but as "practical" symbols. This means that they symbolize sanctification, but with the connotation of the divine intention actually to sanctify this pacticular human being, and to sanctify him according to the symbolism of the rite and in connection with the rite. In other words, a Christian sacrament infallibly symbolizes God in Christ offering His transforming grace and actually sanctifying this disposed recipient through the action of the Church.

That any human symbolic action should thus infallibly signify God as acting and infallibly mediate the divine action is, of course, possible only through the intervention of God, in the act of the "institution" of the sacraments by Christ.

INSTITUTION BY CHRIST

What, then, is the significance of the sacraments being "instituted" by Christ? Such an act of institution is more than a brute historical fact, without any intrinsic connection with the sacrament here and now celebrated. To say that Christ instituted a sacrament means that the rite has its origin in His creative will, so that the celebration of the rite comes to pass by virtue of that will. More specifically, the relationship of the rite to Christ has two aspects. There is the historicojuridical aspect: the will of Christ, that certain apt symbolic rites should symbolize and mediate realities transcending all natural symbolisms and efficacies, is continued in the Church by the Apostles and their successors, and comes to the minister of the sacrament as the law for his will and the norm for his action. There is also the aspect of efficacy: the will of Christ is operative in every sacramental celebration. Since, further, the humanity of Christ became possessed of its salvific power through His death

and resurrection, it is in this death and resurrection, themselves the efficacious symbol par excellence of the divine
salvific will, that the infallible signification and efficacy
of the sacramental rite are ultimately rooted.

By reason of institution, then, with its double aspect, its
double elevation of a natural symbolic action to a supernatural symbolic reference and a supernatural efficacy, every
sacramental action of the Church is Christ's action. It is
His not only insofar as it is an act of cult offered by Him
as Head of the mystical Body in union with His members,
but also insofar as it is an act of sanctification. A sacrament
might be defined from this viewpoint as a visible symbolic
action of Christ in and through the Church, whereby He
configures a member of the Church to Himself.

THE CHURCH AND THE MINISTER

Given this relationship of Christ to the individual through
the symbolic cult action of the Church, we are in a position
to understand two points: the role of the Church in the
constituting of the symbolic action, and the role of the
minister.

It was said earlier that the kind of religious activity we
are dealing with in the sacraments is a symbolizing activity.
The sacraments, that is, are not things "out there" but human
actions which are both symbolic expressions of interior
religious consciousness and symbols of the sanctification
man looks for from God. This is simply to say that they
are signs. It is to say that the putting together, in these
signs, of vehicle, that is, gesture and words, and signification
is first of all an interior spiritual action, and that the visible
symbolic action is the expression, the result, of the spiritual

action. Now, in the Christian sacraments, as was also pointed out previously, the signification is one that is accessible only to faith; in other words, the consciousness constitutive of the sign relationship here and now in a particular sacramental rite is a faith consciousness. Since, further, the sacraments are social cultic symbolic actions or the cultic symbolic rites of a community, the faith expressed in them is the faith of the community, the Church. The sacramental action is thus the sensible symbolic expression of the Church's faith. Because, finally, the faith of the Church as expressed in the sacraments has its origin and norm in the intention of Christ who conceived and determined and revealed the sacramental signification, it is this intention of Christ, mediated by the faith of the Church, that is given sensible expression, accessible, indeed, only to the believer, in the symbolic rite.

The Church, in turn, acts through her minister. The importance of his intention is that it is the link between the exterior rite and the faith of the Church, and ultimately between the exterior rite and the will of Christ establishing the sacramental signification. Thus a series of subordinated or mediated intentions informs the symbolic rite with supernatural meaning and efficacy. If the minister does not need faith, but only an intention, an act of the will, this is because he acts simply as the Church's servant in carrying out the symbolic rite which she wills whose faith and love do not fail.

THE RECIPIENT

The final element of sacramental signification to be mentioned is the recipient and his role. The anti-Protestant polemic of Trent and the post-Tridentine period caused the recipient's part in the sacrament to be viewed simply in terms of causality. A man must remove the obstacles in himself to the sanctifying activity of God; he does this by having a certain intention to receive the sacrament and by cultivating certain moral dispositions. Intention and dispositions are conceived as being purely interior. If the recipient must manifest his intention and dispositions by asking for the sacrament, this expression is viewed as something entirely antecedent to the sacrament itself and as necessary simply that the minister may know that the recipient is interiorly disposed.

This picture of the recipient's role is not entirely adequate. A sacramental action essentially looks to a particular recipient: it symbolizes and mediates Christ's sanctification of *this* man. The person who is baptized is thus a constitutive part of the baptismal action as a sensible symbolic structure. Just as the minister's sacramental action, if it is to be true, if it is to be what it purports and proposes to be, and not an imitation, must be the exteriorization and incarnation of a spiritual intention, so the same action as received by the subject, if it is to be true on his part, must be received not simply materially or corporeally, but precisely "sacramentally." This means that the recipient's submission to the minister's action is not a purely physical submission, but is the symbolic expression of an inner spiritual attitude, namely, his submission to the sanctifying action of Christ as mediated through the visible action of the Church. If his submission does not have this symbolic value, the sacramental sign is rendered false, and the sanctifying work of Christ and the Church is frustrated.

The recipient's role in the sacramental action is, however, not yet fully clarified. By the will of Christ the sacraments have a double supernatural effect. One of these effects is caused by every valid, that is, efficacious, sacrament; this first and immediate effect is clearest in the three sacraments which indelibly mark the soul of the recipient with a "character," a mark or seal, a sign of belonging to someone. The second effect is grace; it is separable from the first, since grace can be lost though the character remains, and the character can even be acquired at the time of the sacramental rite without grace necessarily being acquired. The reason why a sacrament should have two separable effects does not concern us here; it is enough to say that the reason lies ultimately in the nature of the Church as mystical Body. What is of interest at this point is that to these two separable effects there correspond in the ricipient of the sacrament two distinct and separable degrees of self-engagement in the sacramental symbolic action and consequently in the sacramental process as a whole. A sacramental action can thus be either partially or wholly true, partially or wholly fictive. A man can, let us say, intend to receive the sacrament of orders and the priestly powers that the sancramental character brings with it, while knowing that he is freely preventing, by his lack of proper dispositions, the grace of Christ from transfiguring him. In such a hypothesis, his submission to the sacramental action of the minister is the incarnation of a sacramental intention. The rite will thus have that basic truthfulness which makes it valid, that is, makes it the symbolic medium of the divine action that imprints the priestly character and communicates priestly powers. Such a sacrament is, obviously enough, only imperfectly a Christian sacrament, for it is a partially false sign and so cannot be the medium of grace.

VALIDITY AND THE FAITH OF THE CHURCH

Apropos of such a valid but "fruitless" sacrament, a final point is worth raising here. It will help us to appreciate more fully how thoroughly the Church enters into every sacramental rite and how the sacraments need to be seen always as symbolic expressions of the Church's faith and love. The point to be made is that even a simply valid sacrament is possible, it would seem, only because of the living faith of the Church, the mystical Body indefectibly united to Christ its Head. What is meant is this.

It was noted previously that in the descending movement of a sacrament as the symbolic medium of man's sanctification by God, the living faith of the Church plays an essential part. The Church mediates and prolongs Christ's salvific will in the institution of the sacraments by her own living faith and by her loving desire to take this recipient into her life-giving unity, to draw him into that movement to the Father which is her life in Christ.

But the Church enters into every sacrament in another role as well: namely, into the sacrament viewed not now from God's side as it were, but from man's. For it is always the Church that presents the individual man to God and Christ to be sanctified. She impetrates for him the salvation offered him in the sacrament. The sacramental action expresses her response to the divine condescension and her acceptance of salvation for this man who is about to become or already is her member. All salvation is, in a sense, offered and given to the mystical Body, inasmuch as no salvation comes to man except he be somehow united to the Church, the gathering of believers in Christ, outside of which there is no salvation.

The vital role of the Church's living faith is clear in the case of a child. Faced with the problem of how infant baptism could be defended in view of the universal principle that "No one is saved unless he believes," St. Augustine came to understand the justifying power of the Church's faith in this instance in which the human being is not, and never has been, capable of personal faith. This solution of St. Augustine was not a simple speculative hypothesis on his part. It was an insight that came from meditation on the mystery of original sin: "The child believes in the person of another, just as he sinned in the person of another" (Sermon 294. 11. 12). In both damnation and salvation there is a solidarity between the human race and a Head. To the natural and supernatural solidarity of men in Adam, there corresponds the supernatural solidarity of men in Christ, a solidarity actualized for the individual in the mystical Body. The "other," in whose person the child believes, is the Church, whose faith and love, unlike those of parents or sponsors or minister or bystanders, cannot fail. Within the solidarity of the mystical Body, created by the Holy Spirit, the Church attributes its living faith to the child, and by reason of this faith and love God sanctifies the child.

It is true that the Church's faith cannot draw down sacramental sanctification on an adult if he closes himself to grace and refuses to make the Church's living faith his own. But such an adult can, as was pointed out, have nonetheless at least a sacramental intention and thus will that the sacrament be for him in some measure what the Church desires that it be. Then God responds to the faith of the Church by granting to the recipient that preliminary supernatural gift, for example, the sacramental character, whereby the Church receives him, initially in baptism or in some further degree in other sacraments, into her unity, into a situation calling for God's grace. As soon as such a man opens himself fully to the action of Christ, he will be sanctified by reason of the sacrament received.

IV

There are other important points that might be raised: for example, the precise relationship between the objective efficacy of the sacraments and the recipient's faith; above all, the nature of sacramental efficacy and how Christ and the "mysteries of His flesh" are operative in the sacraments. But such matters are rather complicated, and a brief statement might be misleading.

These, then, are some of the basic orientations in the present-day discussion of the nature of Christian sacramentality. This discussion has, clearly enough, profited greatly by the recovery, in Christology and ecclesiology, of certain patristic insights as profoundly meditated upon in medieval theology, and by a deeper understanding of the liturgy as an expression of the life of the Church. It was inevitable that sacramental theology should profit by gains in these other sectors of theology. The sacramental system is too closely connected with redemption through Incarnation and with the Church as the visible presence of Christ in the world, for it to be otherwise.

Whatever be the reason for the development, there can hardly be any doubt that "sacrament" is today a richer concept than it was in the not too distant past. The sacraments are beginning once again to be seen as they were seen by St. Augustine and his Greek peers. They are symbolic actions, heavy with the age-old desires and aspirations of religious man, and adopted by the creative will of Christ to be symbols of the living faith and hope of His mystical Body. In them He offers to the Father, with and through the Church, the redemptive worship of the cross. In them He symbolizes and effects the sanctification of men, uniting them to Himself in His Church and through this union configuring them spiritually to Himself, the Son and the Image of the Father.

In such an understanding of the sacraments there is obviously much that requires further thought and clarification. There is also much that seems to carry with it its own authentication: it turns us at every point to the center and source of Christian life, Christ in His Church.

NOTES

1. The most comprehensive effort at a systematic synthesis is the still incomplete work of Henricus Schillebeeckx, O.P., *De sacramentele heilseconomie* (Antwerp: 'T Groeit, 1952). To this book all who are working in this sector of theology owe many stimulating ideas.

2. The following section owes much, for ideas and for formulations, to the work of H. Schillebeeckx, mentioned earlier, and to his article "Sakramente als Organe der Gottesbegegnung," in *Fragen der Theologie heute* (edd. J. Feiner, J. Trütsch, and F. Böckle; Einsiedeln: Benzinger, 1957). This article is a summary presenta-

tion of his book, *De Christusontmoeting als Sacrament van de Godsontmoeting* (Antwerp: 'T Groeit, 1958; to appear in German in late 1960), which, in turn, is a sketch of the as yet unpublished second volume of his major work.

3. Is there any need to insist, after what has been said in the last two paragraphs, that "symbol" is *not* to be *opposed* to "reality"? The human nature of Christ is no less real for being a symbol, but also no less symbolic for being real.

Herbert Musurillo

>>>>><<<<<

SYMBOLISM AND
KERYGMATIC THEOLOGY

To THE Christian the problem of symbolism has always been a fascinating one: for, since the beginnings of Christianity the symbol has been an all-pervasive feature of his religious life. The area of discussion is, however, a difficult and thorny one. The view I have been developing is that we have perhaps been wrong in the past to cling to either the modern concept of literary genre, which so heavily depends upon Western Rhetoric, or the German notion of *Form*, particularly from the work of Dibelius and the early Bultmann, in our approach to the Scriptures and the literature of the primitive Church.[1] We must, I have suggested, work out a new notion of form based on the practice of the early catechesis in the East and the West. It is, as one may say, a kerygmatic form. This was, in any case, a more concrete notion of form, as we find it in the daily practice of the Fathers of the Church. And this form of the kerygma would, in the last analysis, be a unique fusion of Judaic and Christian (or Greco-Roman) elements. Further, it was suggested, this was to be set against the History-Symbol scale in order to understand historical or dogmatic content. No strict formal definition, therefore, can be given of the Christian literary form save in a very broad sense: thus we have gospel, apocalypse, homily, edifying life, theological dialogue, and all the rest. The particular, individual shape of a work was the result of a very complex set of circumstances. Next, with regard to historical or dogmatic content, each work must be considered on its own merits. A typical example of the problem is Jerome's *Life of Paul the First Hermit*, which was a cause of dispute even in Jerome's lifetime; it is perhaps totally fictional, though it reflects the spirit of early monasticism, especially as it was understood in the West since the dissemination of the *Life of Antony*. The biography of Antony, on the other hand, attributed to St. Athanasius, is based on actual history, however eulogistic and edifying it may ultimately be.

The entire technique of the early catechesis was indeed based on a subtle blend of history and symbolism. The rules for instructing catechumens are laid down in Augustine's *De catechizandis rudibus*, and we may find them implied in Gregory of Nyssa's *Life of Moses*, his *Catechetica magna*,

and his *Commentary on the Song of Songs*. The basic procedure was to sum up all of theology by way of a narrative
called the *historía* (*narratio*): this would include the
religious history of God's dealings with man from the Fall
down to the coming of Christ, concluding usually with
an account of the Last Things. Interspersed with the various
stages, or coming after the actual account, would be the
theoria, the symbolic explanation of the story and the application. The constant preoccupation of these catechetical
texts is: What is the meaning of the story for the catechumen?
Moses' crossing of the Red Sea and the destruction of the
Egyptians, as Gregory of Nyssa reminds us, signify the entrance into the waters of Baptism, and the routing of past
ways and sinful passions. The Western Fathers tended to
be more immediately practical: Augustine explains that after
the narration the catechumen must see that he is to put on
the *mores Christi*, the virtues of Jesus. Many patristic texts
can be explained by reference to this technique. It is the heart
of Augustine's *City of God*, for example. Here Augustine
tells two contrasted stories, that of the City of God and that
of the City of Earth. For each he gives its origins and its
Last End: the one culminates in beatitude, the other in Fire
and the Judgment. Despite the different aims Augustine had
in view throughout the course of this rambling work, its
fundamental structure is dependent upon the catechetical
technique of *narratio*.

The symbolic technique of the early Church, with variations from East to West, comes down ultimately from
Judaism; and its development was strongly influenced by the
Alexandrian school. The techniques of the allegorical
method, which were first applied to the Scriptures by Philo

of Alexandria, were again closely related to the Stoic-Cynic method of interpreting literature of an edifying purpose. How far Christian allegorical and symbolic exegesis was influenced by Philo,[2] and how far by the Greco-Roman or Stoic practice, is still a debatable question. And the controversy has been made more acute since the study of the allegorical and messianic exegesis which seems to occur in the Habacuc Commentary in the Dead Sea Scrolls: here the prophecy of Habacuc is applied to the Teacher of Righteousness. In Philo, we find an adaptation of the nonliteral, or spiritual, interpretations of the Scriptures which were used by the Jewish teachers and are reflected in the *Midrashim.* For Philo, however, the spiritual interpretation is usually philosophical or ethical; and it is this secondary interpretation which Philo refers to as "type," "shadow," "enigma," "mystery." For Philo very often the spiritual interpretation comes into play when the literal, or obvious, one offers difficulty; and many of the Alexandrian Fathers follow him even to the rejection of the literal sense on occasions when they found it "not suitable for God" (*ou theoprepes*). This is the criterion of Alexandrian exegesis, and it extended even to the West in the commentaries of Ambrose, Augustine, and Jerome.

It was from Philo's sense of the "enigma" in Scripture that the Alexandiran catechetical school developed what we now call the fourfold sense: (1) the literal or obvious sense of the sacred text; (2) the Messianic, in which Christ's redemptive work is foreshadowed; (3) the moral or tropological, in which some edifying doctrine is taught for the profit of the Christian soul; and, finally, (4) the eschatological, in which the mysteries of the Final Coming and the hereafter are suggested. Though the Fathers who, like Chrysostom, came under the influence of the Antiochene school, insisted more strongly on the literal meaning, still the possibility of allegory made the scriptural commentary or homily a most flexible and potent instrument for the evolution of Christian dogma. Indeed, as we shall see, the earliest Christian poets instinctively seized on allegorism as a rich source of poetic statement. The tradition culminates in Dante, if he can be considered the author of the Epistle to Can Grande della Scala; for here the entire *Commedia* is interpreted according to the fourfold sense.

But we may perhaps relinquish the problem of origins. Suffice it to say that symbolism and allegorism are at the heart of all Christian literature, beginning with the Gospels themselves. It begins, of course, with Christ's application of the Old Testament to Himself: "starting with Moses and the prophets," Luke tells us, "he expounded to them the Scriptures." In this way He illuminated His messianic mission, following the technique used by Hebrew teachers and rabbis. Any further use of allegorism in the Synoptic Gospels is difficult to prove: unless, of course, we follow Pascal's suggestion that all the healing miracles—in addition to their historic dimension—have a profound relationship to Christ's ultimate mission on earth, the spiritual healing of mankind. Augustine, too, is taken by the image of Christ the heavenly Physician, whose surgical operation cannot be accomplished without great loss of blood, His own as well as the patient's.

But in the strictly literary sense, we first encounter symbolism in the Gospel of St. John and the Apocalypse. In the Apocalypse, an account of a series of ecstatically induced visions, allegory is part of the total texture; the picture of the Lamb enthroned as in a royal court, the Woman crowned with stars, the Harlot of Babylon seated among the seven hills, the King and his warriors on white chargers, the glistening towers of the heavenly Jerusalem. It is perhaps more difficult to analyze symbolism in the Fourth Gospel; even exegetes do not agree on the line where symbolism merges into history, and there is much that is still hotly disputed. Even the figure of the Beloved Disciple himself, around whom so many important events in the Gospel seem to revolve, sometimes seems to suggest the fervent, believing Christian soul, who is at the end entrusted to the love of the Virgin Mother, Mary, who seems to stand, in a sense, for the Church itself. Most, however, would agree that the night which envelops Judas as he goes forth signifies the Power of Darkness. Here we touch one of the recurrent themes of the Gospel: the clash of Light and Darkness. The inaccessible Light of the Godhead has shone on the world in the Person of the Logos; Darkness is the principle of evil, personified in Satan and manifested in the plot of the Jews to destroy Jesus. Again, some symbolism is latent in the gushing of blood and water from the side of Christ on the cross; the most common view would associate it with the new dispensation of grace under the symbol of water as we find it; for example, in Isaias. Indeed, it is the water-grace symbolism that has been suggested, by Hugo Rahner among others, as the real source of the devotion to the Sacred Heart. The water symbolism is clear once again in the episode of the Samaritan Woman. Throughout the Gospel John chooses miracles from the catechetical tradition, but he treats them in quite a dif-

ferent way from the Synoptics. The story of the man blind
from birth suggests the blindness-vision theme—"Blessed
are they who do not see and believe"—and the blind
man's final act of worship has an obvious relevance for
the new converts of the Johannine community. The multiplication of loaves underlines the meaning of the Christian
agape; the miracle of Lazarus' raising from the dead might
perhaps be understood as reinforcing the doctrine of Jesus
as the Resurrection and the Life. The newly baptized comes
forth from the waters of Baptism as Lazarus came forth
from the grave. But here we are on less secure ground.
Suffice it to say that the symbolic potentialities of John's
Gospel are still to be explored.[3]

But the problem of symbolism in the literature of the
primitive Church suggests a further problem, which it is
here our intention to discuss: the complexity and importance of symbolic communication in the religious life
of the Christian in the world today. For the sake of con-
venience we may divide our discussion into four stages:
(1) symbolism and the individual psyche, (2) the problem
of interpersonal communication, (3) symbolism and the
Christian imagination, and (4) the problem of symbolic
theology.

SYMBOLISM AND INDIVIDUAL PSYCHE

Within the past few decades there have been two widely
divergent techniques used to explore the mystery of the
human soul: the various methods of depth psychology
which have been the object of such violent controversy,
and the more recent field of communication theory. It was

in 1938 that Claude E. Shannon, of the Massachusetts Institute of Technology, discovered that electrical circuits could correctly be laid out by using the formulae of Boolean symbolic logic. Within ten years he had worked out a coherent system, and in 1949 with Warren Weaver he published the monograph which was to become the foundation stone of all future work, *The Mathematical Theory of Communication* (University of Illinois Press). Shannon himself has emphasized how much his theory owed to the work of Norbert Wiener in the field of Cybernetics, but this would be beyond the scope of the present discussion. What concerns us more is the fact that communication theory, in addition to its utility in the construction of electronic computers, has had far-reaching effects in every area of human expression and communication, in every field in which language forms the medium of growth and development.

Before discussing the possible areas of contact between symbolism and Christian philosophy and theology, it may be useful, by way of preliminary, to explore the basis of symbolism and communication, that is, the complexity of the human psyche.

The importance of symbolism lies in the drive that all men have to express their inner experiences and to communicate them with the outer world. Thus the complexity of the symbol in any age is a function of the complicated drives and needs of the human psyche at any given moment in history and in accordance with the culture in which a man may find himself. Thus before treating the problem of interpersonal communication we must first discuss symbolism as an expression of the individual's needs.

The clue to man's psychological life is transaction. Biologically speaking, the individual is a selfish organism, moving, growing, developing throughout its life span by a fixed internal law. It perfects itself by a constant despoiling of the environment, by a continuous adaptation in accordance with its life needs. In this sense, each independent principle of life is a law unto itself; so that, when the organism expresses itself, it reacts upon its environment somehow in accordance with its internal drives and needs. Man's environment is predominantly sociometric: he is psychologically orientated toward other men, with the result that the social dimension constantly colors and modifies all his drives and motivation. But physiologically and psychologically it remains true that each exists for himself. There is truth in the old adage *homo homini lupus*—a truth which Hobbes grossly distorted in the development of his political theory. But from the purely biological point of view human altruism remains somewhat of a mystery.

In any case, by its very nature the individual human psyche is the autocratic control center that governs all transactions: it is the ultimate receiver, transformer, and transmitter of all the complex signals that form the continuous current of communication with the outside world. This continual stream of information is to the human soul what the bloodstream is to the heart and tissues. With the constant relay of signals there is constant adjustment to the changing environment, and periodic feedback (or storage of useful information for future needs). Some of the incoming signals become conscious, others not. Predominant among the conscious signals—as opposed to stimuli of the automatic nervous system—are those which require the organism to make complicated psychological adjustments: those that involve decision and choice. Now to assist in making this decision the human soul has at its disposal a vast reservoir built up since birth: ideas, images, memories of pleasure and pain, instinctive and learned patterns of behavior. The elements of this stock exist in various states covering an entire spectrum from the conscious to the unconscious. And all are tightly interwoven in what has been called an associative pattern. The laws of this vast spectrum have just begun to be discovered; and lists of psychological mechanisms have been drawn up. Some of the most frequently discussed mechanisms—that is, patterns which seem to operate in the soul's use of its psychological storage —are projection, identification, transference, rationalization, and the like.

In reacting to this environment, man thus manipulates a highly complex organization which includes his conscious intentions, the psychological storage which has been the result of feedback, and, finally, what we have referred to as his drives or needs. Some drives are always present to a greater or less degree though they do not always demand immediate satisfaction. Of the more permanent drives there are the basic body needs for food, sleep, procreation; and the host of other human security drives, such as the need for love and respect, achievement, the need to grow in our understanding of ourselves and the world, and so on.

But, it seems, the complex pattern within the human soul is never perfect. The dynamics of interaction among all these elements are such that, in certain men at least, there is psychological degeneration of the sort that prevents the psyche from adjusting properly to its environment. There is, in short, human bewilderment, eccentricity, deviate and criminal behavior, neurosis and psychosis. Indeed, even the so-called normal individual, living today in the presence of a constantly growing flood of information, lives on the borderland of anxiety and confusion. But even Martin Heidegger, who has perhaps given us the classic portrait of *Angst* in the modern world, speaks with more coldness than sympathy. Heidegger is more like the aloof magistrate pronouncing judgment that the sympathetic beholder of confused humanity. He castigates man for his *Neugier*,[4] that effusion, dissipation, and distraction that is the daily life of so many men and women. What he overlooks, among other things, is the simple bewilderment that all of us suffer from, the result of so many conflicting images, ideas, impressions. It is something like the electronic computer that has been fed simultaneously contradictory instructions. The machine breaks down.

Particularly in the area of morals, many men, no matter how conscientious and sensitively aware of their obligations, find life not only confusing but psychologically painful. Whether its source is the world within or the world without, all good men are sometimes immersed in an atmosphere of indecision, remorse, scruples or doubt, insecurity and fear—fear for ourselves or for those whose lives may be bound up with ours. Not only do we experience the Pauline conflict: "The evil that I would not, that I do"; a sometimes more painful and acute condition arises from not knowing what is to be done, or, after discharging what we thought was our duty, doubting that it was the best course. It is a paradox that the most fervent Christians are precisely those who are most tortured with that vice that has plagued the modern world, scruples.

In the past, man's highest activities, art, philosophy and religion, have been therapeutic: they have attempted to help him adjust to his environment, and to reach an equilibrium wherein he would be at peace with himself and his fellow man. Yet today there is so much discussion of pure art, pure philosophy, and so on, that there is real danger that these may become areas of specialization appreciated only by an elite. No science or art should become so autonomous as to be completely divorced from the actual needs of man within his environment. In particular, the modern Christian philosopher and theologian should be aware that not the least of his functions is to bring the message of Salvation to men of goodwill.

THE PROBLEM OF INTERPERSONAL COMMUNICATION

One of the most fascinating of all studies is man's attempt to get in contact with other men by means of symbols. In the area of interpersonal communication, a symbol is the manipulation of spatiotemporal media in order to express or communicate internal experiences in accordance with human needs. Hence they are used to translate psychic experiences into physical phenomena of the sort that would be received and decoded by other men. The symbol situation may exist in three modes: the *gestural*, which develops into music, the dance, and the drama; the *artificial*, in which solid forms or sketched designs are used to convey meaning; and the oral, or *linguistic*, which is perhaps the most recent in man's cultural development. A

possible fourth mode, the *electronic*, may perhaps be the
only way of communicating with rational organisms on
other planets or galaxies; but it will then be merely an
extension of the third mode. I have discussed the first three
modes in some detail elsewhere. But it seems important to
emphasize the fact that in the history of Christianity it is
the first mode, the gestural, which earlier played the
predominant role. God taught His people in the Old Law
by gestures, by dramatic parables, by striking rituals, and,
above all, by the symbolism of events. These great scenes
from the Old Testament, such as the March out of Egypt,
the Manna in the Desert, the inscribing of the Commandments on stone, and so on, were nothing less than dogmatic messages telling of God's special providence over His
creatures. And as such were they used by the Fathers of
the Church, especially in the theoretic exposition (*theoria*)
of the sacred history.

As a development of the gestural symbol and, in particular, the dramatic parable, we have the historic event
symbolism of the New Testament. Events like the An-
nunciation, the Temptation, the Multiplication of Loaves,
the Raising of Lazarus, may well be considered in this
category; for, in addition to their historic quality, Christian
tradition has attached a certain dogmatic and doctrinal
importance to these events in the order of revelation.

Artifact symbols and linguistic symbols are obvious from
the name. Indeed, historic Christianity has had recourse to
all three types of symbolism in its tradition, its liturgy
and its theology. But the symbolic function of theology
as communication we shall leave for discussion further on.

The basic situation we have been attempting to portray

is the relationship between two human beings involved in communication as Sender and Receiver. In this symbol situation the tension arises from the reciprocal attempt to achieve one or more of four aims: (1) to establish an intelligible channel for communication; (2) to express one's ideas, feelings, and so forth, in accord with one's drives and needs; (3) to attempt to influence the other to act in accord with one's own needs; or (4) to attempt to arrive at some collaborative process for the mutual satisfaction of drives and needs. There are, of course, many variants and combinations of these basic aims. But in all cases it should be recalled that the relationship is a binary one: communication is from a definite Sender to Receiver in a definite, concrete context. Information is sent only so long as it achieves its purpose, or is mistakenly thought to achieve its purpose, and then it is broken off. The Sender will attempt many ways of achieving intelligibility (technically called "redundancy") and of avoiding equivocation. But here two remarks must be made. In real life, it would seem, no symbol situation is ever perfect; thus symbols are by their very nature ambiguous. Secondly, they become more ambiguous when they are removed, by quotation, from the concrete context in which they originally arose. Removal in time and place can make a message completely unintelligible.

To sum up, therefore, our remarks on the symbol: it is always concretely anchored in space and time; it always has a binary relationship within the communcation context; it is fundamentally ambiguous and liable to equivocation or error.

Now in addition to the purely functional aspects of communication as suggested in the first and second of the four aims listed above, symbols are constantly being used by men to influence their fellows, that is, to cause them somehow to act in accordance with personal demands or needs. It has taken many centuries to learn that though stones and animals may yield to physical force, the highest human aims can be achieved only by words. In the Western world at least, it was the Greeks who first became skilled at the art of diplomacy, and the first rhetorical manuals were written by three Sicilian Greeks, Corax, Tisias, and Gorgias, who taught at Athens in the fifth century. In any case, the discovery of the power of the spoken word had deep implications for the future history of thought. But the exact source of this power has always remained something of a mystery. Gorgias and other Greek thinkers seem to have located it in some sort of magical spell that the trained speaker exercises over his audience; and they connect it with the effect music and poetry had on the emotions and passions of listeners. It is in this way, they claimed, that words can heal the wounds of the soul, much as medicine healed the body, and music calmed the mentally ill. Indeed, whether or not this view really derived from primitive magical beliefs, it seems in any case at the heart of much of the didactic poetry that was so popular in ancient Greece and Rome. Literature, like music and medicine, should also have its therapeutic effect on man's soul.

But the problem of rhetoric or persuasion in human relations remains a puzzling one. Is it possible by symbolic communication to manipulate other men, to cause them to act in accordance with my own drives, needs, whims? And, if it is possible, how far is it desirable that we should do so?

As for the first question it is clear that men can be influenced to act, but only, it would seem, when the action is somehow subservient to their own internal psychology, to their own ideas, desires and so on. But what then are the ethics of persuasion? What means may we use in our communication to bring about the desired response? Let us consider the various ways in which this end is achieved. In the first place, there may be the simple presentation of the case as it actually exists, with whatever emotional tone it may possess. When after this presentation no action ensues, we are usually aware that our needs do not correspond with the dispositions or drives of our listeners; hence we go a step further. We first try to describe the situation in such a way as to make it appear to correspond to the existing needs of our audience. There is, at this stage, a certain distortion of the truth. And, if this does not produce results, we proceed to create in our listeners the specific drives that will issue in the desired action; we arouse emotions or passions, by our message, that can only be calmed or satisfied by the performance of what we want. This is the usual course, it would seem, of persuasive speech; it is the regular path followed by advertising based on motivational research: either show how your product satisfies a need—or else create the need. Now it would seem that, apart from the normal emotions aroused or evoked by a sincere discussion of needs, any procedure that distorts reality for the purpose of moving men to action is immoral. The conclusion seems so clear as to be inescapable. And once accepted, it has far-reaching conclusions in all areas of human thought and discussion, in philosophy as

well as theology: we may not distort reality for the purpose of producing results which we deem desirable.

THE ADVENT OF CHRISTIANITY

The achievement of Christ has produced a distinct change
in the relationships among men and, consequently, in their
mode of communication. The earliest apostles were by the
mandate of Jesus messengers or witnesses to announce the
Good News (*evangelium*) to all men. Their message was,
as we capture it in the first chapters of the Acts of the
Apostles, the proclamation (*kerygma*) that the Messianic
Atonement had been accomplished by the Servant of
Yahweh according to Isaias the prophet; that Jesus had
died, risen and gone to His Father; and that all men should
be baptized in His name and communicate in His mysteries
until the end of the world. Thus, the primitive *kerygma* was
a special sort of communication by those who had been witnesses of the redemptive mission of Jesus. It was not a
coercion, but a simple, sincere message charged with the
emotional conviction of those who had "seen, beheld, and
handled concerning the World of Life." This primitive
kerygma and *didache*, the former to designate history and
doctrine, the latter the moral implications for men, is the
fountainhead of all theology and liturgy. Liturgy is the concrete cult expression of our adherence to the historic fact
of Christ's Atonement; theology is man's attempt to discover the finite symbolic means of expressing the implications of God's intrusion in history. Theology will always
entail tension, imperfection, and constant growth in man's
struggle to bridge the gulf between revelation and language.

SYMBOLISM AND THE CHRISTIAN IMAGINATION

The specifically Christian form of communication will, as I have suggested, necessarily be cast into a unique mold. All of man's psychic powers will be brought to collaborate in transmitting the Christian message in a manner that will be intelligible to others. Thus arises the problem of the various forms or modes of expression: art, the liturgy, theology, philosophy. To those men who have come under the sway of the primitive Christian message there arises a new set of internal drives and propensities; the organism, with its storehouse of images, ideas, memories, and so on, has been profoundly modified. It is not to be expected that a man, when reacting to his environment in a Christian way, will be completely indistinguishable from all the rest.

Insofar as symbolic communication is, in great part, the product of the projective or creative imagination encoding or transforming psychic experience, it follows that the imagination will always have a deep influence on any presentation of the Christian religious history. For the Fathers and early theologians the acceptance or rejection of the imagination was a crucial problem; and it is a dilemma that is still with us. It is a problem that is not easy of solution, and one that will have wide repercussions throughout our theology and philosophy. But it may be said at the outset that there can be no question of acceptance or rejection: a man's imaginative creativity cannot be long checked or suppressed; it is a human drive that must somehow emerge and have its way. We can do little more than plot its course and observe its function in all areas of human life. Man must be somehow accepted as he is.

What is, however, a more fruitful question is: Can we speak of a specifically Christian imagination, and, if so, what is its function? Is a Christian art possible, or should we rather speak of an art that happens to be practiced by Christians? To this question I believe a more positive answer can be given, based on what we know historic Christianity to be.

Even from the psychological point of view it would seem that there is, or at least should be, a specifically Christian imagination, one, that is, that has been elevated by Baptism into the Mystical Body, and has been impregnated by the truths, symbols, and liturgy of Revelation. However, the imagination of the artist or thinker need not always operate in a specifically Christian way; and thus it happens that what Christians produce in the area of art, or philosophy even, is hardly distinguishable from the work of non-Christians. But the Christian imagination, when it is working in its specific function, is concerned precisely with the tension, the polarity, which arises between visible, sensuous reality and the hidden things which have been revealed to us, between the phenomena of time and the substance of things hoped for.

It took the early Christians some centuries to work out the possibilities of an art or a literature that could exist apart from catechesis and liturgy. Nonliturgical poetry, for example, had a most difficult existence. In the first place there was the problem of the adaptation of secular, pagan techniques to the needs of the growing Church. But why should the Christian write poetry at all when the means of salvation lay close at hand, in the Church and in the Scriptures? It was, I think, Paulinus of Nola who was the first to carve out a Christian theory of art and poetry. His famous tenth poem, written as an epistle to his former teacher Ausonius, puts the early Christian dilemma as well as it has ever been expressed. Ausonius, himself not too fervent a Christian, had urged Paulinus to resume his interest in poetry. And he replies:

> You urge me, Master, to take up again
> The Muses I have long abandoned. But why?
> Hearts pleadged to Christ are closed to Apollo,
> And deny entrance to the goddesses of song.

And he continues:

> Another force, now, a greater God
> Urges me, demanding a new life,
> Claiming of us a sacred duty.

But it is clear that, in the very writing of this new Christian verse, he is settling the problem that vexes him. The very tension and conflict that he speaks of are precisely the stuff of Christian poetry; and as Paulinus says finally:

> Indeed, what the eye sees is but passing;
> Invisible are the things that are eternal,
> Glimpsed only in spirit and embraced by hope.

This then is the source of the authentic Christian artistic vision: the tension between the supernatural and the tangible cosmos in which we are immersed. Sometimes there will be clash and seeming contradictions, when the brilliance of this world's light only heightens the shadow of faith, and all seems ambiguous and obscure. Yet, at other times the world of the Transcendent seems to complement the visible, and the universe is seen as a forest of symbols that can be deciphered only the eye of faith. This is the dilemma, buried deep in the unconscious of the Christian, that is the wellspring of any specifically Christian art, literature or philosophy. Of the role of philosophy we shall have something to say further on. But it seems clear, in any case, that if the role of theology is to express and develop in humanly intelligible symbols the message of Christian revelation, then it is the province of art and literature not merely to repeat these solutions, but rather to express the reaction of the Christian imagination to the newly awakened conflict of human existence. Truly great Christian poetry, therefore, will often speak not of peace but of contradiction.

THE PROBLEM OF SYMBOLIC THEOLOGY[5]

Theology is the reiteration of the primitive kerygma by the Mystical Christ in the concrete, developing context of time and space. As it reiterates and explains the Good News, the Church makes the message clear for the particular age and time. Her voice, therefore, the *auditus fidei*, is a continuous signal to the minds of men, at once communicating, preserving and, by that very act, developing the content of the primitive message. The original communication must remain the same; and yet somehow there is intrinsic in the historic nature of man the propensity for development. But in the case of the primitive Christian

message, we are not yet able to theorize on the potentialities for growth nor yet on the laws that govern this historic
phenomenon.[6] It is the task of the theologian to determine
the limits and progress of dogmatic communication, and
to explore the structure of revealed truth. The preacher of
God's word to the people, on the other hand, does not
speculate or explore, he does not coerce or cajole: he is
merely the Church's messenger, the modern witness of
Jesus, in the deliverance of this urgent message of salvation.
It becomes clear, then, that the minister of the Gospel, as
the preacher of the Word, must avoid any display of
theatrical rhetoric of the sort that would ill suit his
prophetic role. In the primitive Church the homily was
more closely bound up with the Liturgy, especially with
the catechesis. Though it is not so today, the ideal of the
Christian preacher ought still to be the lovely vignette, preserved in Luke (4:16 ff.), of Jesus preaching the acceptable
year of the Lord in the synagogue of Nazareth. Here there
are no histrionics: it is an announcement, a simple statement of the facts. Modern preachers of religion, influenced
perhaps by the techniques of the modern dynamics of
persuasion, by entertainment or advertising media, even
perhaps by political oratory, have lost sight of the symbolic
mode of communication which is the proper role of the
messenger of the Word. How far modern homiletic practice may borrow from the handbooks of persuasion and
motivational research, is for the specialists to discuss. In
any case, the homily, so intimately a part of the Liturgy
in the past, must be identifiably Christian; it may not be
a Stoic diatribe or a political address. The preacher is always
the servant of theology in mediating God's truth to the

people. He is a mere mouthpiece, a voice; and his message, though now transformed to become intelligible in the present, should not be substantially different from the message of primitive Christianity.

In relation to our present inquiry, however, it will be the task of the theologian to explore the historic progress of the Christian communication and its relationship to its primitive expression. Theology determines the exact relationship of history to symbol in this expression, and the status of the various components of the message as it exists, concretely, today in the living Church. Symbolic theology, therefore, will have as its function the exposition of the different types of symbol that occur in Scripture, in the liturgy and, in particular, in the sacramental system.

A science of symbols within the Church, as it moves through these three areas, can be either descriptive or comparative. A comparative symbol theology would discuss general religious symbols as common to many faiths, noting what scholars and psychologists have solidly established. Some of this field has already been begun by writers like Jung, Mircea Eliade, Gerald Vann, and Jean Daniélou. Here the area that Daniélou has called cosmic liturgy and cosmic religion should be perhaps more fully explored. But in many respects it is a difficult and unrewarding field, because the sounding of man's unconscious, at least in the area of comparative religious symbolism, is such an uncertain and precarious task.

But the path of historic-descriptive symbolism should be a smoother and more objective one. In our treatment of Scripture and the liturgy, however, we must emphasize a point that has not always been observed in the past.

Symbolic communication in the liturgy and in the Scriptures are two specifically different kinds of symbolism, and must therefore be handled quite differently. Symbolism in the Scriptures, where it occurs, is literary and linguistic; that of the liturgy is gestural and dramatic. The Scriptures, in the first place, are a document; hence we must be careful that we have understood their meaning *as a document* before we can discuss the symbolic dimension. It is a trap that is quite easy to fall into. Thus, in discussing a passage of Scripture, let us say the book of Judith or Tobias, a preliminary question must first be answered, and answered ultimately by the scriptural exegete under the guidance of authority: How far are Judith and Tobias to be considered historical figures? What is the tone and intention of the work as a document? Only when we have answered this question may we go on to explore the symbolic intentions of the sacred books under discussion. Thus symbols in Scripture are never on the same level as those we observe in the liturgy.

Further, in a scriptural event that is historical, as, for example, the Crucifixion, the symbolism is an added, though important dimension; and, once again, it is of a different sort from the symbolism of details in Scripture which are not, or were not intended to be, fully historical in the strict sense. The symbolism of the marriage of Yahweh and His people in the Song of Songs and in Psalm 44 is linguistic and literary, the result of the sacred poet's artistic as well as divine inspiration, and has parallels in other religious documents; but the symbolism that may be attached to Christ's prayer and fast in the desert must begin with the fact that the sacred writer is, in this case, recording history.

In every case, of course, analysis of symbols can proceed only under the guidance of competent Scripture scholars.

SYMBOLIC CAUSALITY IN THE LITURGY

The discussion of symbolic communication ultimately leads us to that most difficult of all questions, the nature of sacramental causality. Here again communication theory may throw new light on this age-old question. The problem is narrowed down, however, if we consider the entire liturgy as a species of *gestural* symbolism, like bodily movements which signify, like the drama and the dance, whether or not they are accompanied by words. The entire liturgy is, in truth, one vast corporate gesture in which all the faithful participate in varying degrees. The washing by water is, of course, the entry rite, the signal by which a man obtains the approval of the Church and the right to participate. The Mass itself is the archetypal sacrament, the focal act of participation and incorporation of the baptized into Christ and the Church. All the others cluster around these as gestures of special sacred significance for those who have been sealed with the blood of the Lamb.

The key, then, to sacramental causality is the redemptive act of Jesus and the significance He wished to be attached to it. The Cross is the historic expression of man's reconciliation with God; and as an act of vicarious satisfaction and sacrifice it is the effective cause of man's redemption in the spirit of the second Servant Song of Isaias, chapter 53. It is by a study of Isaias' doctrine that we can see how the death of Jesus has become a vicarious sacrifice; it was such because that was what He intended it to be. His historic gesture would not only signify redemption by sacrifice; it would achieve it. It is thus that, in the Cross, History and Symbol become one. In the Last Supper Jesus established a ritual which by word and gesture, and by implicit reference to the Jewish ritual, symbolized the act of Atonement and at once gave the outward sign by which men could participate in its effects. The causality of the Cross is both supernatural and historicosymbolic.

The celebration of the mysteries of the Lord, "until He shall come," becomes now a channel of distribution of the graces of the Atonement; and its causality as a liturgical ritual of commemoration must be analogous with the effectiveness of the Atonement itself. The Mass, as a memorial ceremony, as a narrative that tells of God's redeeming Gesture, not only symbolizes, it also achieves; and its causality is also historicosymbolic, though of a secondary order. The causality of the Church in the liturgy is corporate and mystical, though mediate, dependent and secondary.

So it is with all the other sacraments. They are all, in a sense, the mysteries of the Lord, commemorative of His life on earth. They are all in their special ways symbols of participation in the graces of the Redemption, and, as such, their causality, though corporate and physical, is secondary and derivative. As symbolic gestures which dispense the graces of the Atonement they have a threefold reference: to Christ, to the Church, and to the individual participant. As rituals shared in by the faithful, they are tokens of decision, of assent and union; as sacred gestures of the Mystical Body the sacraments are signs of the Church's willingness to adopt, to incorporate, to reconcile the faithful soul in the specific way achieved by each sacrament; and, as ancient rites and formulae, they are cues to devotion and prayer as well as evidence of the Church's historic bond with the primitive catechesis and liturgy which came from her Lord.

The Christian preacher, then, must constantly remind himself of the unique, prophetic nature of his role. As Augustine clearly saw, in his discussion *De doctrina christiana*, the primary aim of the preacher is *docere*, instruction, communication, and not *persuadere* and *placere*, to persuade or to give pleasure. Whether or not the message of the Church pleases our audience—though as the Good News it should—is strictly irrelevant to our mission. For the rest we must make sure that our communication is understood and, indeed, that we understand it ourselves.

Augustine's four books *On Christian Doctrine* are the first treatise on the problem of symbolism and kerygmatic theology. In the first two books Augustine is at pains to distinguish between signs and things: signs are the means men use to communicate with one another, and so the language of Scripture constitutes a special complexus of signs; through signs we are led to things; and through things to God. Thus in the first part of the work Augustine attempts to explain the importance of the liberal arts and sciences in order that the Christian preacher might understand both signs and things. In the third book, Augustine applies this knowledge to the comprehension of the Scriptures; and in the fourth book he discusses the mode of communication which the Christian teacher must use. Ultimately, however, the central thesis of *On Christian Doctrine* is: God's message can be communicated only as it has in the past, by a definite sort of symbolic communication. However, we must set this statement against the general background of Augustine's thought: that only by Wisdom can a man come to a full understanding of the truth that is in the universe, and of the message that is communicated in the sacred writings. For Augustine this faculty of Wisdom is not wholly a cold, intellectual process: it is an act of the whole man functioning in virtue of the divine image that he bears within him—*memoria, intellegentia, voluntas*—operating under the impulse of grace, the *delectatio victrix* which confirms and supports the good within us and helps check the evil.

In accordance with Augustine's analysis, all of us, and above all the preacher, the Christian messenger of the Word, must bear in mind that theology was from the outset a communication to *men*, a message to the soul of man to listen to the Good News of salvation. It was ultimately a message of peace and encouragement; as the lovely medieval Easter hymn tells us:

> Death and Life
> Have met in mortal strife;
> Our Captain, dead, still reigns
> As Lord of Life.

Theological theory, therefore, should never grow so abstruse and obscure in the lecture halls as to lose its contact with the ultimate problems it was intended to solve. Jesus' life and death were not a drama performed so that the Platos and Aristotles of the world should sit and pass judgment on it. "I came that they might have life, and have it more abundantly."

To this kerygmatic character of theology, which is indeed not by any means its total function, the Christian philosopher has, in the past, given his support. Though independent in method, authentic Christian philosophy has not stood aloof or uncommitted in the battle that has raged over the soul of man. For the philosopher, like the artist, in his specific function as a Christian, has always attempted to explore the tensions that arise in man precisely because of the Christian revelation: the polarity between Immanence and Transcendence, between the soul in time and immortality. Though in the realm of pure reason, if we may use the term, he may not be different from his non-Christian colleagues, yet acting as a Christian, and calling upon his own vast conscious and unconscious store that has been the result of the Christian message, his task will always be to explore precisely those avenues of reality that have been opened by the challenge of Revelation. His precise function, therefore, is a positive one: it is the exploitation of Wisdom in the Augustinian sense under the inspiration of the hierarchic Church.

From the kerygmatic point of view, the message of Christian philosophy and theology has always been one of human hope. In man's historic struggle for self-mastery, the Church has always encouraged him to enhance and support those spiritual ideals that have ever lured him onward. The suggestion one often encounters in reading non-Christian historians, that the Church has constantly tended to thwart man's progress on earth, finds no support in the history of Christian theology. Indeed, the meaning of Salvation as the Church preaches it to man today, is, in no small part, the confident assurance that man will always have at his disposal all the supernatural, otherworldly means to help us calm the conflict that is within us, to reach an equilibrium that is essential for Christian living. Only in such an atmosphere can man devote himself wholeheartedly to the arts, to the sciences, to the works of peace. Again, in support of the Gospel message, the philosopher has always maintained that man is free, against all those who would reduce human activity to necessary, irresistible drives; and, finally, that man's self-determination is rooted ultimately in his ability to perceive transcendental values and in his awareness of his strength to attain them.

Finally, against the modern leaning toward a phenomenology of death in the spirit of Heidegger, the Christian philosopher has always maintained that man is not a prisoner of the physicochemical universe, and has offered him some basis for belief in immortality. Man's very ability to explore the universe is in itself a token of the destiny promised by the Christian *kerygma*. For truth, ultimately, is one. As Augustine has said in his treatise *On Christian Doctrine*, "all truth is the Lord's, no matter what the source." All truth is Christian, however veiled under transient figures and obscure symbols. To discover the Godhead hidden therein is the highest function of a Christian philosophy of symbolism.

NOTES

1. See especially "History and Symbol: A Study of Form in Early Christian Literature," *Theological Studies* 18 (1957), 357-386, with the relevant literature there cited. Cf. also the criticism of these views by Jacques Dupont, *Les Béatitudes* (2nd. ed., Bruges-Louvain, 1958), pp. 18 ff.

2. For a thorough discussion of Philonic influence on Christian allegorical methods, see H. A. Wolfson, *The Philosophy of the Church Fathers* (Cambridge, 1956), pp. 24 ff., though he cannot perhaps be followed in his conclusions with regard to Paul and the early Fathers.

3. See, for example, C. H. Dodd, *The Interpretation of the Fourth Gospel* (Cambridge, 1953) p. 142: "The Johannine *sêmeion* . . . refers . . . to timeless realities dignified by the act in time." For Dodd, every miracle-sign in John points forward to the great climax, that is, to Christ's work of giving Light and Life by the historical act of His death and resurrection. Dodd, of course, is at the opposite pole to the extreme views adopted by Bultmann and his school.

4. See *Sein und Zeit* (8th ed., Tübingen, 1957), pp. 170 ff.

5. For an introduction to the problems involved, see Gerald Vann, *The Paradise Tree: On Living Symbols of the Church* (New York, 1959). See also the important article by Karl Rahner, "Dogmatik," in *Lexikon für Theologie und Kirche* (2nd ed., Freiburg, 1959), III, 446-454.

6. See the sound conclusions suggested by K. Rahner, "Dogmenentwicklung," *Lexikon für Theologie und Kirche*, III, 457-463, although he can suggest (col. 462) no ultimate solution.

Francis J. McCool

>>>>><<<<<

THE PREACHER AND
THE HISTORICAL WITNESS
OF THE GOSPELS

WE ARE fortunate to live in a period in which theological activity is livelier than it has been in many a day, but perhaps no department of theology has recently undergone such sharp changes as the study of Sacred Scripture. Awareness of this fact has now inevitably penetrated beyond the narrow circle of those engaged in research. It has reached the members of the clergy and, indeed, the Church at large. As always, news of change has called forth varied feelings among those whose own lifework precluded participation in this particular enterprise. The word has gone around that the Bible must be read "in a new way," and, above all else, that is not as easy to discover the meaning of the Gospels as earlier and more ingenuous generations had believed. Some of these reports are enthusiastic exaggerations, but beneath the exaggerations there remains a substratum of sober fact which needs to be faced.

This is all the more necessary because these reports have shaken the confidence of some priests in their ability to perform an essential part of their ministry, the preaching of the word. These men, most of whom received their theological training before 1943,[1] seriously wonder if what they think they find in Scripture and particularly in the Gospels is really there. Is the method which they were taught to apply to these writings seriously at fault? And if so, what steps can they take, granted the obligations of their present life, to remedy the situation? A state of affairs which evokes questions such as these merits the most serious consideration. It is obviously impossible in a single essay to provide the preacher with answers to all these perplexing problem. However, a consideration of one of the most serious psychological hazards occasioned by these new developments, i.e., an honest attempt to state it, analyze it, and judge its validity, may be as good a place to tackle this problem as any. However incomplete the attempt may be and however tentative its conclusion, this first step may be of service in helping the preacher understand just what one of these "changes" with regard to the Gospels implies and why the exegete feels that this change should help rather than impede the preacher in his work.

The particular hazard we have chosen to treat is general in nature and concerns the nature of the Gospels as historical sources. It is the assertion, held so commonly by exegetes today that it has now found its way into the textbooks of Introduction to the New Testament, which affirms that the Gospels can no longer be considered as "pure" historical sources.[2] Here, unfortunately, is a point where rapport between exegete and preacher is not nearly as close as it should be. The preacher finds this statement shattering,[3] yet many an exegete cannot for the life of him see why this should be. How can the preacher, he reasons, feel that the truth of his message is imperiled by what is being proposed by exegesis on this point? Surely he is aware that he receives his message, the Christian revelation, from the Church? And does not that same Church assure the preacher that the sacred books in which a great and important part of that revelation is contained are inspired and are thus protected from error? Therefore, concludes the exegete, whatever my work may reveal about the nature of the historical witness furnished by the Gospels, the preacher must be aware that he possesses and will always possess a certainty passing that of historical science that what the Evangelists intended to express and succeeded in expressing in their works is absolutely true.

But while this is certainly true of the preacher *qua* believer, the exegete should not fall under the illusion that this chain of reasoning will remove the present difficulty. The preacher, despite his faith and his office, remains a man and as such lives in a definite milieu whose viewpoints and values he appropriates quite unconsciously. Now no one can deny that our age is historically minded, that it places a higher worth on the results of historical research and sets higher standards of historical accuracy than was true in the past. It is impossible that the attitudes of the modern preacher should be unaffected by this state of affairs.[4] Like any other child of our times, he wants to know the past accurately, to see it re-created *wie es eigentlich geschehen*, especially when that past touches him so closely as does the life of Jesus. Secondly, the preacher has been formed by a definite training. He was instructed in his seminary quite as thoroughly as the exegete in the irreplaceable value of Christian faith and the unshakable security it should afford him. He is equally conscious of the implications of the doctrine of scriptural inspiration. But he was also told that his acceptance of the Christian revelation should never be a leap into the void with eyes tightly shut, but, on the contrary, that though based on the authority of God, this act should be both reasonable and prudent. It is precisely here that the preacher feels that the modern view of the historical witness of the Gospels fails him. Confronted with it, he is tempted to reason as follows. The life of the Son of God on earth is the heart of the Christian revelation, and the main historical sources for that life are the four Gospels. Therefore, if the Gospels are not reliable sources, how can my faith be ever reasonable or prudent?[5] But if the Gospels are not purely historical accounts; i.e., if they expressed what the early Church believed took place in the years of Christ's life rather than what actually happened, how can I trust them? The preacher is quite aware that it is not his function to establish the historical worth of the Gospels. He is content to leave that to the historian of Christian origins, the exegete, and the professor of apologetics. But he insists that their historical trustworthiness is a truth which must be established for him by reasons he can understand and accept before he can devote himself with peace of soul to his own work. What is bothering him at present is that the exegetes apparently have undermined the process by which his professors established this truth for him and have given him nothing with which to replace it.[6]

PURE HISTORICAL SOURCE

Before answering these questions directly, it will be well to examine this concept of "pure" historical source which the preacher feels must be predicated of the Gospels if their accounts are to be considered reliable. The concept, strange as it may appear, is relatively recent in origin, having been formulated by the German school of history which flourished during the last century, the historico-critical school. Founded by Ludwig von Ranke (1795-1886) and Theodor Mommsen (1817-1903) and brought to a climax by Eduard Meyer (1885-1930), the ideal of this school was to create a historical methodology which would treat its subject matter as objectively as the natural sciences. Like the physicist and chemist, these men strove to see the past unmoved by the passions and controversies which its decisive events still arouse. They wished to reconstruct as true and complete a picture of what had actually taken place—*wie es eigentlich gewesen*—as was humanly possible.[7]

The writing of so exacting a type of history naturally demanded a careful evaluation and sifting of historical sources. In composing his histories of Europe in the sixteenth and seventeenth centuries, von Ranke had discovered a category of primary source which was particularly adapted to his purpose. These were *Urkunden*, i.e., official documents contemporary with the past events, and luckily for von Ranke the archives of the chancelleries of Europe were well stocked with them. Those which were particularly helpful to him were found in the Venetian archives, where the reports of the various ambassadors of the Città della Laguna had been preserved. These were accurate, detailed, dispassionate accounts, based either on the personal observation of the envoys or on what their trained judgment had found credible in the information supplied by their agents. Von Ranke rightly judged these accounts to be as reliable a historical source as any historian was likely to discover. His experience showed that they distorted the facts far less than the accounts of those who had been closely involved in those great events or of historians who sought literary laurels. So, after examining his *Urkunden* carefully, he rested much of the great histories he composed on the data they furnished him. Now von Ranke's works were more than merely successful; they were rightly judged to be masterpieces of historical writing. Their success consequently canonized the ideal of the "pure" historical source, i.e., an account of the past set down by onlookers who sought to be precise, detailed and above all else objective.

As luck would have it, this ideal of history and its "pure" source was developed in precisely the age and country where the historical study of the Gospels was most intense. The influence of the Enlightenment was felt everywhere in Protestant Germany, and many of the brightest spirits in Lutheranism were encouraged by it to free themselves from the "bonds of outdated dogma" by going in quest of the "historical Jesus."[8] In these circumstances it was inevitable that these two currents should converge; indeed, they fused so inextricably that the von Ranke ideal of history and a modified form of his methodology still dominate biblical criticism whether Protestant or Catholic. As we look back on the past, we see that this influence has been both beneficial and harmful to biblical studies. As Albright remarked: "It is obvious that, whatever happens to future history, scholars must always be profoundly grateful to the men who were the first to recognize the supreme importance of accuracy and completeness, both in defining facts and in explaining changes."[9] But if the ideal undoubtedly led to great advances in the science of history, the enormous success of the method canonized by that ideal in the field of European and classical history was not always repeated when applied elsewhere. For its very success tempted epigoni who were not gifted with the historical tact of the master to attribute universal applicability to this particular way of studying the past and therefore to apply woodenly the methodology which had been fruitful in rediscovering one or two ages to the history of every land and time. The belief began to be held that, if a historical source was not "pure," it was not very reliable.

This generalization had grave effects in the field of biblical criticism, where the stage of historical action was the Ancient Near East during the millennia covered by the Old and New Testaments. As far as the New Testament was concerned, the unimaginative application of what came to be called the historicocritical method resulted in a ceaseless series of judgments all of which tended to discredit the historical worth of the canonical Gospels. From the very start of the process scholars became aware that one of the Gospels at least failed to measure up to the ideal of the "pure" historical source. This was the fourth Gospel, which was soon unanimously judged to be lacking in this regard and therefore—and here was the fatal error—was held to possess little, if any, value as a source for the history of Jesus. Looking back a trifle ruefully on this period, Anton Fridrichsen, a leader in the modern Scandinavian school of exegesis, summed up the historicocritical school's rejection of this work in vivid terms:

To an older generation it seemed self-evident that the Gospel of St John must be regarded as altogether secondary to the Synoptic Gospels. The life and teaching of Jesus are to be found in the Gospel of St Mark and in the logia-source of St Matthew and St Luke. In St John we do not find history, but a theological construction on the basis of, and with its starting-point in, certain Synoptic motifs. The Evangelist aimed at describing the work and teaching of Jesus, His death and Resurrection, in forms and language which appealed to his own religious outlook and experience. Consequently Jesus speaks St John's own language and proclaims his thoughts. The narratives are saturated with Johannine Christ-mysticism and Johannine speculation; they have a double basis, since a symbolic and allegorical character has been added to them which has nothing to do with authentic history. Everywhere the theological reflections of the Evangelist, or of the Johannine circle, obtrude themselves; and when in certain indirect allusions he [the Evangelist] pretends that the Gospel was written by one of Jesus's disciples and most intimate friends, this is a literary artifice to confer the highest rank and authority on the book. Thus the Gospel of St John does not belong to history except as a factor in, and an original document for, the history of dogma. The Evangelist, or his circle, has de-

veloped Pauline theology further towards mysticism, has purified its language from all Judaism, and subordinated it to the
universal scope of the Greek notion of the Logos.[10]

The effects of the two influences we mentioned, the dis-
taste of the man of the Enlightenment for dogma and his
acceptance of the von Ranke "pure" source as the only
reliable basis for scientific history, pervade the above paragraph, in which the testimony of the fourth Evangelist was
waived completely out of court. Despite his transcendent
claims, which are an integral part of the historical record,
Jesus was placed on the same level as any other individual
of the past, and an attempt was made to write His history
on this basis. The source texts which came under scrutiny
were valued to the extent to which they provided "authentic
material," reliable biographical data, i.e., the words which
Jesus actually pronounced at the various points of time
described in the sources, and the events as they appeared
to the bystanders at the moment of their occurrence. Any
theological constructions which were placed on the facts,
i.e., the use of symbolism, the interpretation of prior events
in the light of events which happened after the human
career of Jesus, the use of categories other than those employed by the Master Himself, were excised from the
record on the plea that such have nothing to do with
"authentic history." Furthermore, because he was not a
Rankian before von Ranke, the fourth Evangelist was
judged to have had no contact with Jesus' intimate friend.
Because he expressed the teaching of the Lord in his own
words and forms of thought, he was paid the great but
dubious compliment of being considered the author, not
only of the expression, but of the thoughts themselves.

Despite the recurrence of the phrase "Johannine circle," both Master and Evangelist were imagined to have existed and worked in the individualistic manner characteristic of post-Renaissance man, and no attention was really paid to the bonds of tradition which might possibly have bound them together. Fridrichsen's judgment is echoed by many moderns: "This critical view of St. John's Gospel is based on patent facts. But have the right conclusions been drawn from them?"[11] What was responsible for this completely negative judgment of the historical worth of the fourth Gospel was neither St. John nor the work of accurate analysis performed by the scholars of the historicocritical school. What was wrong was the absolute reliance on one kind of historical source and the mechanical transfer of the methodology associated with it from one definite period of history to another which differed widely from it.

However patent it may appear to us, this truth was not immediately evident to the scholars of the nineteenth century. The entire second half of that century was devoted to seeking the "pure" historical source which would surrender the authentic data which finally they, the men of the Enlightenment, would interpret adequately.[12] As the quotation from Fridichsen makes clear, the canonical Gospels of Matthew and Luke were also found to be defective as "pure" sources, although the sentence of condemnation was never so strongly phrased as in the case of John. As a result, the historian was reduced to two "pure" sources: the Gospel of Mark, which provided the only historical account of Jesus' actions, and the famous Logia or Q, which alone reproduced His teaching accurately.

These two documents provided the basis on which the

Liberal school of theology attempted for forty years to recover a Jesus whom they could understand and revere without invoking the dogmas of the past.[13] It was because of this double presupposition, i.e., that the combination of the philosophy of the Enlightenment with the historical skills of the nineteenth century had *de facto* recovered the true Jesus of Nazareth, that the Liberal school was shaken to its foundations in 1901 by Wrede's demonstration that dogmatic ideas had shared in the shaping of the Marcan Gospel. Wrede's book forced them to admit that, far from being the "authentic record" they had imagined it to be, the Gospel of Mark, as its title had always proclaimed, was in its way quite as theological as the fourth Gospel. What made the work of Wrede appear so negative to the Liberals that it caused them to despair was not that he had proved, as he and they thought, that the second Gospel was unhistorical. What Wrede had proved was rather that the concept of the "pure" historical source which the historicocritical school had canonized fitted Mark no better than the other Gospels.

At this juncture Form-Criticism entered the picture. If the fourth Gospel, Matthew, Mark, and now the two documents which lay behind the common Synoptic tradition were all found to have been "contaminated" by theological interpretations, the only hope of finding the Jesus of history on the presuppositions of the historicocritical school was to sift the oral tradition which on Luke's admission had been the point of departure of the entire process. But the work of the Form-Critics only confirmed what earlier scholars had found to be true of the later stages of the gospel tradition. Each of these forms or genres,[14] be they "prophetic and apocalyptic sayings," "interpretations of the Law" or "rules for the community," "Christ-stories" or "Jesus-stories," presented the Master, not as He had appeared to the half-opened eyes of contemporaries, but as seen in His full dignity by Christians, i.e., by those who had accepted Jesus' testimony to Himself, His work, and His nature.[15] With all the possible material for research thus exhausted, the truth began to dawn on scholars: either the "pure" historical source was not an absolute requisite for the writing of "authentic history," or they would have to abandon all hope of knowing the Lord Jesus by means of that science. They would have to be content with the Christ of faith. This is the dilemma which also faces the modern preacher who insists on a "pure" historical source. For if there is one point which the work of these many years has established for all, Catholic and Protestant, it is that none of the Christian sources for the life of Jesus which we possess can be so denominated.

Although many scholars chose and are still resigned to the second alternative, to be content with the Christ of faith,[16] others began to wonder if the impasse was not attributable to the method employed rather than to the sources. Despite the merits revealed by the von Ranke method in elucidating the Reformation period in Europe, was it the only way in which scientific history could be written in our age? Or—and this conclusion was nearer to the truth—was it neither the sources nor the method which was at fault? Was it not rather that substantials had been confused with accidentals, with the result that the method was being applied quite unimaginatively to the history of Christ? It is Fridrichsen again who shows us what these men had been ignoring in their routine application of von Ranke's method to the Gospels:

Gradually, however, the conviction has grown that this is not the way to study and interpret ancient Eastern religious documents. An Israelite prophet or a Jewish Messiah cannot be understood solely in terms of Western thought in the nineteenth century. The man of God is never isolated. He is always the centre of a circle taught by his words and example, in which his manner of life and teaching continues after his death. What is taught and written in this circle is ultimately derived from its founder and embodies his life and character. When we, the children of a later age and of another culture, wish to understand such a person and his period, we must return to tradition and inquire there; but our inquiry must be made with due understanding of local peculiarities. Only with such a sympathetic understanding is it possible to estimate a tradition as a source of history. No appreciation can be acquired without insight into the habits of life and thought of prophetic circles in ancient Israel, or of Jews of Rabbinic education and Messianic outlook. It will become clear that tradition is an excellent source for history, if the history we have in mind is the conduct of life in associations governed and influenced by persons who in some extraordinary way speak with divine authority. But it will soon also be found that no biographical or psychological account of such figures can be given. They cannot be viewed as individualists in their consciousness or their behaviour; their souls are of quite a different structure from those of modern European men. Real understanding is only possible after considering the legacy they leave to their circles, and the tradition formed, preserved and continually propagated within them. This of course does not imply that in principle one is to refrain from isolating earlier and later strata within a tradition, or from determining as far as possible, by critical observation and reflection, facts and utterances immediately associated with whatever person is the object of research. But it means that one cannot hope in this way to study the character of a prophet as a modern historian would. No conception of him can be formed except by observing how he was remembered, described and quoted, and what was handed down about him. All these things form a totality of which he was the soul, because he did not keep his soul to himself, but gave himself to those who received his words, his nature and his will into themselves. Therefore, from the point of view of what is demanded in a modern biography, any statement concerning men of God in the ancient East must appear extremely unsatisfactory, uncertain and fragmentary as an exercise in biography or in character study. But to one who has liberated himself from the narrow view and limited experience of the Historico-critical School, tradition itself in all its abundance, variation and multiplicity will be the mirror in which historical reality is reflected. What has here been stated in general terms is relevant to a long line of Biblical persons, to Isaiah and Jeremiah as well as to Jesus and John the Baptist.[17]

Let us insist on one thing here: Fridrichsen is not lowering in any way the high standard for scientific history set by Ludwig von Ranke. Equally with that scholar, he wishes to know the history of Jesus, *wie es eigentlich geschehen*. He, too, will strive to explain how that particular history came to pass, *wie es eigentlich geworden*. But he is at once less dogmatic and more modest than other followers of the great historian. He admits in practice what the sources emphasize: the special nature of the central figure of this history ("a man of God in the ancient East") and the peculiar conditions of the stage on which He acted His part. Moreover, he will permit the circle around Jesus to interpret their Master to us, aware that Jesus rather than His followers is the source of what they say, even though they may formulate it in their own way. But, above all else, Fridrichsen is aware of the nature of historical method and of the danger of transforming it into historical dogma. He denies all absolute value to any particular historical methodology, no matter how refined it may be, and insists that the methods which the historian employs must be adapted to his sources and not vice versa. If no "pure" historical sources are discoverable, then the historian must seek out the possibilities for "authentic history" proffered by the sources in existence. These may not be those he would like to have, e.g., the witness of uncommitted onlookers. They may rather be a tradition formed by those "who received his words, his nature and will into themselves." He realizes as a scientific historian that this type of source will be quite difficult to handle, for the preoccupation of his authors will differ from his. But he will not abandon them for all that; he will create tests to determine the measure of historical accuracy contained in the statements of his witnesses. The tradition may not strive to answer the questions he would like to place. He will note what it considers important, and he will be content if his particular interests are partially satisfied. This attitude of Fridrichsen and others, more open, modest, but scientifically quite as rigorous as that of his predecessors, has replaced the frustration caused by the work of Wrede and his fellows, and it has set moving a new quest for the historical Jesus.[18]

This new quest is, if anything, more difficult than the preceding one, but the very awareness of the difficulties involved makes it more circumspect and safer. Recognition that the developing tradition which embraces our Gospels in its sweep can be "an excellent source for history" is only the first step in a long and arduous process. The scientific historian must first show that the tradition he uses is authentic, i.e., it derives ultimately from contemporaries of the events and was set down in an honest attempt to present what the Master said and did. A careful study of the contents, the mode of transmission, and the intention displayed by those involved in producing our Gospels has made it certain that our four canonical Gospels substantially belong in this category, whereas the apocryphal gospels, globally considered, belong with equal certainty to the category of pseudo tradition which is defined as "the result of an intentional fabrication of history." This justifies the *presumption* that any pericope in our Gospels is broadly speaking historical and allows the historian to advance to his second stage.

The historian's second step involves classifying, weighing and determining the exact historical value of the various elements which form this authentic tradition. This does not imply any doubt as to the trustworthiness of any particular pericope, for all belong to what has been shown to be authentic tradition. But the very notion of a growing tradition and a brief examination of the gospel material combine to show that this authentic tradition is not all of one piece. First, despite the brief space of time which elapsed between the resurrection of our Lord and the first Gospel, analysis of the Gospels reveals that the tradition crystallized in them contains elements belonging to earlier and later strata. Secondly, all these strata contain a variety of forms or genres. Since none of these forms intend to express the event or saying to which they bear witness in strictly historical statement, as that phrase is understood today, the historian must determine the precise intention implicit in the original form and that revealed by the particular use which the Evangelist has made of it. This done, he must decide the extent to which these two distinct intentions have influenced the statement in his text, and in the light of those considerations judge exactly what can be deduced from it concerning the event or saying in the lift of our Lord which is being reported. This is a delicate business, which can be safely accomplished only by a formed historian who has been trained in the evaluation of ancient texts generally and of the Gospel texts in particular.[19]

PARABLE OF THE SOWER

We shall realize the need for a trained observer fully only if we see the process in the concrete. Let us take, then, the well known parable of the Sower and follow the historian as he studies it. He approaches his task with a double hypothesis firmly held in mind. The first of these he derives from a general study of the Synoptic Gospels, whereas the second is the result of a careful investigation of the entire New Testament. In order to see what is implied here, let us enumerate some of the judgments that are contained in each of these complex hypotheses. The first, which is based on the Synoptics, concerns the concrete historical situation created in Palestine by the appearance of Jesus of Nazareth. This involves definite judgments about the nature of Jesus' activity on earth, i.e., that His preaching was eschatological, salvific, exclusively religious, and challenging.[20] Based on these, further judgments concern the relationships His

activity created between our Lord and those with whom
He came into contact (His adversaries, the people in
general, His disciples), the quality of these relationships
at various points of His career, and the general lines along
which they developed. Thirdly, judgments derived from
many texts pertain to more particular aspects of Jesus'
being and activity. For example, His language is presumed
to have been Aramaic, His way of expressing Himself concrete, popular, Palestinian; His persevering use of parable
is conceived to have been directed to the purpose to which
that genre tends by its nature. What we have termed the
first hypothesis is, therefore, a whole chain of tentative
judgments, resulting from controlled observation, each of
which combines with all the others to form the mosaic
which reveals to the observer an approximation of what
Jesus' life was really like.[21]

And this is only the first hypothesis. The second of these
two hypotheses concerns a distinct historical situation, that
of the Early Church after the events of Easter and Pente-
cost. It involves judgments about the activity of that
Church, the scope of that activity—be it kerygmatic, catechetical, liturgical—and its purpose: tending to conversion,
instruction, exhortation, prayer. Besides these, this hypothesis contains definite judgments about the relationships
which existed between the Church and normative Judaism,
the various fringe sects, the Jewish people in general,
proselytes, pagans. In addition, judgments about the methods
employed by the Christian community in mediating the
traditions about Jesus belong to this second hypothesis, i.e.,
the interests which lay behind this activity, the literary
forms it inherited, modified, or created in the service of

those interests, the theological terminology in which it expressed itself. All these various judgments are assented to with various degrees of probability or certitude according to the strength of the converging elements which sustain them. Before he turns to his text, therefore, the historian is in possession of a body of knowledge concerning the two points which are most relevant to his inquiry: the period of the public life of our Lord and the period in which the Church was enshrining her memories of the Master in durable form.

Presupposing this background which will provide the criteria for his future judgments, the historian turns to his particular text, the parable of the Sower.[22] But first he will note the context in which this story is found in the Gospels. The Sower is not preserved as an isolated parable but is set at the head of a chapter where a number of related parables appear.[23] All these parables, with the exception of the Sower, treat explicitly of the kingdom of God. Moreover, they all describe various organic processes more or less according to the same pattern. They contrast two stages in an organic process, the initial and the final, the little mustard seed and the great shrub, the small amount of leaven and the batch of bread which the leaven causes to rise, the passive husbandman and his sudden activity at the moment of harvest, the period when grain and weeds are allowed to grow together and the moment when they must be separated.[24] Thirdly, his knowledge of the Old Testament makes it easy for the historian to identify the point of time in the history of salvation connoted by the second stage of the parable. The great shrub which gives shelter to the birds of the air is a traditional image for a

great kingdom.[25] The images of the harvest and the husbandman putting in the sickle evoke the eschatological
moment, the end of time and the judgment.[26] It is, therefore,
clear to him that the moment Jesus intends the second
stage of these parables to represent is that so ardently hoped
for by the Jewish people. It is the moment when the glorious kingdom would be inaugurated and God would close
His accounts with His people. These parables, therefore,
belong to the eschatological preaching of Jesus.

In addition, the identification of the final stage leads the
historian to what our Lord intended the first stage to represent. He recalls the aspects of that stage which the parables
present. The mustard seed is small and insignificant, the
leaven adds the note of hidden activity. The inactivity of
the husbandman is what is stressed in the first half of the
Grain Growing Secretly. The Tares insist that at first the
weeds must be allowed to grow together with the grain.
In addition, the historian recalls that the idea of growth or
process, which underlies all these parables, relates and
contrasts all these aspects of activity or inactivity with a
definite point of time, the moment when the kingdom will
come in glory.[27] These observations, together with the
knowledge of the nature of Jesus' preaching gained from
His background, naturally lead him to identify the first
stage of each of these parables with Jesus' own ministry,
which had given rise to messianic hopes and yet seemed in
many ways thoroughly unmessianic.

For the contrast between the hopes Jesus caused to rise
and the way He conducted Himself was a burning problem in our Lord's lifetimes. Because of it, the Baptist had
permitted himself to ask: "Is it thy coming that was fore-

told, or are we yet waiting for some other?" (Matt. 11:3). Jesus had answered him indirectly, by reminding him of the prophecy of Isaiah (*ibid.*, vv. 4-5). And now the parables of growth answer the same difficulty with a different reference, but in the same elliptical manner. The Jewish people had expected that the future kingdom would be glorious, but Jesus, despite His acts of power, appeared to them at times quite ordinary. They had thought that the coming of the kingdom would completely change the conditions of this world, yet the world went on very much as it had previously, although Jesus was there. The Jews undoubtedly wondered why Jesus did not use the means for establishing His Kingdom which were obviously practical in that period, i.e., the force recommended by the zealots, or why He insisted on being on friendly terms with sinners, instead of creating a "pure" community as the Essenes of Qumrân had done. Jesus answered all these expectations, as He had in the case of the Baptist, with a challenge to observe and reflect. Look at the mustard seed, the leaven, the grain growing secretly, the tares, and note above all to what they lead. "The apparent smallness and insignificance of what is happening does not exclude the secret presence of the coming kingdom. . . . The lesson of [these parables] is thus, not so much the great results of the work of Jesus, as it is the 'organic unity' between his ministry and the future Kingdom of God."[28] These are parables of contrast, but underneath the contrast there is unity.

The historian has noted that Matthew and Mark had placed the Sower at the head of the chapter in which these parables were preserved. This leads him to compare this parable with the members of the group. On examination, its structure appears to be analogous to theirs. Here, too, a first stage in a natural process is contrasted with the ultimate: a single action is described which was initially unsuccessful, but ultimately extremely effective. Moreover, as in the other parables, the richness of the harvest is a familiar Jewish symbol for the eschatological kingdom.[29] However, stress is laid in this parable on the aspect of failure to an extent not found in the others. Nevertheless, as the parable expresses but two contrasting ideas, these first three images (birds, etc.) must be taken as variants of the theme of failure. Moreover, despite the emphasis on failure, the main stress of the parable is not placed there but on the final stage. Both its position and the exceptional triple yield[30] indicate that here the story reaches its climax. Structure and imagery, therefore, combine to suggest that this parable, like the others, is meant to convey a definite aspect of the mystery of the kingdom of God.

If the parable of the Sower thus interpreted fits easily into the picture which the historian had previously constructed of Jesus' ministry in Palestine, the same is true of the vocabulary and literary genre exemplified by this pericope. The vocabulary of these few verses points unmistakably to a Semitic background. The use of the definite article where we should favor the indefinite (Mark 4:3, 4, 5, 7, 8); the phrase *para tēn hodon*, which chose the weaker alternative of the ambiguous Aramaic *'al'urha*; the secondary Semitisms: *anabainein* for the springing up of the corn (4:7, 8) and *didonai karpon* (4:8), all indicate that "the Greek version of the parable in Mark stands near to an Aramaic original."[31] In addition to this, the Sower appears to be an example of pure parable. It relates a simple fact of daily experience with the utmost naturalness and accuracy. One detail alone, the richness of the ultimate yield, is abnormal, and even this is extraordinary rather than miraculous.[32] Nothing here suggests an allegory whose details are expressed in a cryptic, metaphorical language which should be interpreted one by one. Rather, this parable, is a series of concrete pictures that combine to indicate a single lesson which the hearers could discover by reflecting on the concrete historical situation in which they found themselves.

Nor was discovery of this moral beyond the capacity of the famous "man on the street," if he only attended to the story. Every element in it, structure, imagery, and the symbolic climax, answered the question which was upsetting Jesus' hearers: How could He be Messiah, the bringer of the kingdom, if He acted as He did? Just as the Sower, Jesus' initial lack of success will not prevent His work being ultimately crowned with glory. "The start has been made and nothing can prevent the coming of the kingdom"—this is the fundamental assurance given His hearers by this parable.[33] It is, therefore, fundamentally good tidings, a gospel message. However, the emphasis on present failure cannot be denied—the birds, the rocky ground, and the thorns will not slip from memory. More than in the other parables of growth, Jesus is facing up to the unfavorable aspect of His present ministry. His appeal is failing, the moment of grace for His hearers is quickly slipping by. They must attend, take heed, and believe, for their share in the kingdom is at stake. This parable is, therefore, also an exhortation. From what he knows of the course of Jesus' activity, the historian can form a fairly accurate idea as to when such a parable would have been spoken. It would fit neither at the beginning nor at the very end of His ministry. Jesus spoke it when the initial enthusiasm had faded away and when some of His hearers walked no more with Him. However, His voice does not have here the tone of bitter regret we hear in His last days. It seemed as if the divine plan of salvation might permit the falling away of many, but there was still hope, so Jesus raised His voice in warning and in promise. The point of time indicated here is, therefore, well on in Jesus' ministry. As to the place where the parable was spoken, nothing that we know about Jesus' way of preaching, nor even the time element suggested by the message, would cause the historian to dispute the testimony of all three Evangelists that the parable was spoken in Galilee. Therefore, he inclines to date the parable as thus interpreted towards the close of the ministry in Galilee.[34]

However, this is not all which the Gospels offer about the parable of the Sower. In each of the three Synoptics an interpretation is appended which is attributed to Jesus Himself. Here is an element which calls for careful assessment, for its preservation shows that it possessed importance for the Early Church. The first impression made on the historian when he studies this application is that its general sense is different from that which he had derived from the Sower in the light of the other parables of growth. The interpretation does not speak of the kingdom but of Jesus' word. Moreover, its message is this: just as the harvest yield depends on the fertility of the ground in which the seed is placed, so too the effect of Jesus' word is proportioned to the dispositions of His hearers.[35] Of course, the interpretation, like the parable, is more than a piece of simple exposition. It, too, is a warning: the disciple must not be content with having heard the word of the Master; he must assimilate it and make it a principle of practical living. Secondly, the manner in which this message is conveyed by the interpretation surprises the historian who has studied the parable. Jesus explains the parable as if it were an allegory, taking each individual phrase and giving its explanation. Moreover, the historian is astonished by the clumsiness of expression here. Jesus explains that the classes of listeners resemble the *seeds* that fall on the various parts of the field, whereas He clearly means that they were like the different kinds of *soil* in which the seed had been placed.[36] In addition, he wonders why Jesus places no stress in His interpretation on the final details of the story. The threefold yield is mentioned but not developed. As Jesus explains it, the story possesses no climax to speak of, the impression being given that the last stage is, if anything, of less importance to the commentator than the earlier ones.[37] Finally, the difference in vocabulary between parable and interpretation arouses the historian's interest. Parallels to the words and expressions used here are not to be found in the Gospel texts which have been judged on intrinsic grounds to approximate the *ipsissimae voces Jesu*, but in the New Testament epistles which have preserved for us the categories and formulae of the Early Church.[38] An additional fact is that this passage, in contrast to the parable, contains no Semitisms nor does it hint in any way that it is "translation Greek." This interpretation, which contrasts in so many ways with the story it sets out to explain, rather than helping the historian to understand the parable, provides him at first sight with a tantalizing problem.

The only means to solve this problem at the disposal of the historian is to relate the contrasting phenomena to his general knowledge of the Synoptic Gospels, the nature of Jesus' Palestinian preaching, and the purpose of the Early Church in forming and preserving traditions about its Master. The Synoptic Evangelists, he is aware, did not compose their works in one relatively continuous effort, as modern authors do, but were content to edit material selected from the mass of testimony about Jesus which had crystallized into fixed form at various points of time in the thirty years which separated Mark from the events he reported.[39] As for Jesus' Palestinian preaching, his researches have convinced the historian that it was essentially a heralding of the coming kingdom, which, to be effective, was necessarily conditioned by the concrete historical situation of that ministry. Thirdly, it is evident that the aim of the Early Church was practical rather than scientific. In forming the gospel tradition, it strove not for precise historical statement but rather to represent truly the entire activity of Jesus in a manner which would also reveal its relevance for its adherents and their contemporaries.[40] Seen in the light of these considerations, the most reasonable explanation of the contrasting phenomena seems to lie in attributing parable and interpretation to different strata in the developing tradition. As every element about it suggests, the parable belongs to a very early stratum, probably not more than two removes from Jesus Himself. The interpretation, on the other hand, gives evidence of belonging to a later stratum and appears to reflect the vocabulary and above all the *Problematik* of the Early Church rather than that of Jesus' Palestinian ministry.[41]

Unlike some of his predecessors, the modern historian will not let the matter rest here. He feels bound to explain plausibly why the Early Church should have so restated this parable that Jesus' word, i.e., the Christian revelation, replaced the kingdom of God as the center of interest, while attention was transferred from the unity between Jesus' ministry and the coming kingdom to the external and internal obstacles which could prevent that revelation obtaining its desired results. He finds that the explanation of this transposition may well have been given in a second pericope, also of later provenance, which immediately precedes this explanation in all three Evangelists.[42] Here Jesus reveals that He spoke in parables to the crowd in order that the mystery of the kingdom might be preached in a manner consonant with the divine plan of salvation. And this, as Isaiah had made clear, included His own rejection by the Jewish people. In this pericope the Church expressed its awareness of three facts: (1) that "the central message of these parables [of growth]" was "the eschatological significance of the earthly ministry of Jesus," (2) that the parables expressed this significance in a "germinal form" which stated "the secret presence of the kingdom in the preaching and healing activity of Jesus," and (3) that it itself understood this truth in a much clearer manner, "in the form of an explicit christology, with its center in the message of the death, resurrection and heavenly enthronement of Christ." As a result of this possession, "the germinal form of this message . . . was to a certain extent superseded and no longer actual; the parables could find new applications."[43] This is precisely what the analysis of the interpretation had suggested to the historian; in it the writer was not envisaging the Jewish audience to which Jesus first addressed the parable, but rather the difficulties experienced by His contemporaries in putting into practice what the Christian revelation demanded of them.[44]

The all-important question here, of course, is: Does this transposition falsify the original meaning of the parable? It is hard for the historian to see how it does. Despite the crucial omission of any mention of the kingdom and the changed reference given to the element of extraordinary fertility in the interpretation, the balance between the eschatological and hortatory elements has shifted only slightly from parable to explanation. In both, the hortatory element is implicit and the earnest appeal which the Church makes in the interpretation shows that she speaks with a consciousness of her own eschatological situation. Nor has the Church's interpretation changed the dominant intention which our Lord had in mind when He pronounced the parable. Both parable and interpretation implicitly demand a personal decision from their hearers to change then and there the religious and moral attitudes which they had assumed toward Jesus' person or His word.[45] in the parable Jesus uttered this challenge: Believe in me. Despite the apparent failure of my mission, I am He who, as my words and acts imply, will establish the kingdom, and only those who are united to me will enter it. In the interpretation, the Church applied His words to the temptations which those who had heard His word must face. Implicit in its exposition was the appeal to its children, Jesus' disciples, to overcome these threats to their salvation and become

like those who hear and welcome His word. These only
"will yield a harvest, one thirtyfold, one sixtyfold, one a
hundredfold" (v. 20). What, then, has the Church effected
by this transposition? Jeremias has described the change
admirably in treating of a series of interpretations added by
the Church to another of Jesus' parables: "Nothing had
been added to or taken from [the parable]. The accent
has been shifted because of the change in audience."[46]
The shift in interest from the moment when the kingdom
of God will come to the present trials faced by the
Christians gives the interpretation a timeless quality and a
note of personal appeal which makes its mixture of warning
and promise fully applicable to any period in the age
of the Church. The Church, therefore, has not changed
Jesus' message; rather, it has faithfully reproduced it in the
exact form in which Jesus spoke it in the last moments
of the "old aeon" and applied it for the benefit of her
children who must live their lives in the "new age."

His analysis of the interpretation of the Sower is, therefore, far from leading the modern historian to deny historical interest to the Early Church or to accuse it of
substituting its own message for that of the Master. The
manner in which the Synoptics treated the parable-preach-
ing of Jesus rather induces him to attribute to them a
double preoccupation, both of which may be justly termed
historical. They clearly wished to reproduce accurately the
manner, contents and effects of Jesus' preaching in Palestine. Equally strong, however, was their desire to explain to their contemporaries why Jesus had chosen this
manner of preaching and to show the relevance which
that preaching still held for them. This double purpose,

to recall and interpret, and to interpret by calling on Jesus' own words wherever possible, seems to explain best the blend of elements which form these chapters. If either aim might be said to predominate, it was that of accurate recall. This was the reason why Mark carefully informed his readers that Jesus had preached to the Jews mainly in parables, which neither they nor the disciples understood, a fact which led Jesus to instruct the latter specially, because of their providential role. It was surely to preserve the memory of what Jesus had actually said that Mark selected from early tradition three model parables, to which Matthew added others in his turn. Yet both Evangelists felt that accurate reproduction was not sufficient to ensure full appreciation of the message of the Master. So they cited His own words to explain why He spoke as He had— that the divine plan might be fulfilled—and by so doing communicated their realization that, although adapted to the mentality of the Jews, this manner of preaching was an approximation rather than the full, clear statement of what Jesus wished to convey. Therefore, it could only be temporary.[47] In addition, because Jesus had necessarily spoken this parable in a way conditioned by the particular historical situation in which He then stood, and precisely because they had reproduced "this germinal form" of His message as exactly as they could, the Evangelists were eager to show their readers that this parable still possessed relevance for them, despite the fact that the "mystery of the kingdom" had been revealed to them. So they took advantage of a fact which they had to report, namely, that during His public life Jesus frequently explained His parables to His disciples, and used it to insert a traditional interpretation which was in accord with the intentions of the Lord and yet pointed His message so that it applied to the conditions of their own, very different age. The modern historian does not find anything in this procedure which he would term "unhistorical," prepared as he is to allow the Evangelists within limits to establish their own norms for historical writing, instead of imposing on them those of his own time and place.[48]

EXEGETE AND PREACHER

Let us return finally to the preacher, for it may appear that we have forgotten him entirely. This is not so, for one of his major preoccupations about modern exegetical developments has governed the construction of this entire paper. It has tried to state concretely the reasons why the exegete today willingly admits that the Gospels are not "pure" historical sources. He does so, first, because the research of more than half a century has shown that the attempt to qualify the Gospels in this way is chimerical, since all efforts to do so have resulted ironically in establishing that the Gospels and the tradition from which they sprang were composed "from faith to faith."[49] Secondly, the exegete makes his admission without regret, because he believes that research has shown that such sources are not an essential requisite for writing authentic history, and that the dichotomy between what "the Church believed took place" and what "actually happened" is not as irreducible as many have believed. He feels that his own experience and that of his fellows has shown that the gospel tradition composed in faith is a valuable source for history and that, subjected to methodical analysis, it can lead the investigator to accurate conclusions concerning what Jesus actually did and really was. Therefore, it seems to him that the basic reason for the preacher's concern, that denial of the "pure" historicity of the Gospels involves the admission that history cannot provide a basis for the prudent acceptance in faith of Jesus as our Redeemer and Lord, is being resolved *ambulando*.

Nevertheless, the exegete is fully aware that the historical reconstruction of the life of Jesus on the basis of the gospel tradition is not easy. He is certain, besides, that he and his fellows have not completed this task. A start, however, has been made. It has been demonstrated that the canonical Gospels, *in globo*, reproduce authentic tradition. This is important in that it permits a presupposition that what the tradition alleges to have happened actually did so, though the fact in a particular instance may not have been established with historical rigor. But what has yet to be done is more important. This is to determine the exact historical data that can be drawn from each of the multitude of pericopes which the Gospels contain and to correlate this data. Moreover, the nature of the tradition, as revealed by his research, has made the exegete aware of the fact that, even when this task shall be complete, many lacunae will remain which he should like to be able to fill. He regrets this fact, but it seems to him insignificant in view of the many advantages which his new vision has given him. For this has enlarged immeasurably the material on which he can legitimately draw to construct his image of Jesus. No longer restricted to the Synoptics, nor to the earliest strata of their tradition, he can subject the entire sweep of the gospel tradition to his research. And he is more than willing to communicate the results of this research to the preacher as his work progresses.[50] For he knows that in this, even more than in past ages, his work is an essential prerequisite for the fruitful preaching of the word of Christ. But that it may be this, the exegete is aware that the preacher must trust him, his purpose, his dedication, and his skills. He is not surprised, to be sure, that at the present moment this trust may be lacking in some quarters, for he recalls that Pius XII had foreseen this.[51] His hope, however, is that his unfinished work may not be rejected unexamined in the name of principles of doubtful value. It seems to him that the injunction of St. Paul is as relevant today to the exegesis of the Gospels as it was to first-century prophecy: "Omnia probate," the Apostle advised, "quod bonum est, tenete." And for the exegete, the Pauline "omnia" includes not only his own work but also the "principles" which we all have received from an age which has passed away.

NOTES

1. The Encyclical *Divino afflante Spiritu* was promulgated on Sept. 30, 1943.

2. This is equivalently stated in the following description of the nature of the historical witness borne by the Synoptic Gospels: "Nos évangiles sont donc des documents vraiment historiques. Mais comment le sont-ils? En effet, il y a histoire et histoire. La présentation du fait évangélique n'est pas désintéressée, elle est doctrinale" (X. Léon-Dufour, in *Introduction à la Bible* 2 [Tournai, 1959] 328. Cf. *ibid.*, A. Feuillet's pages on the fourth Gospel, pp. 666-671, esp. pp. 670-671.

3. This effect is often due to the failure of the preacher to realize the qualified meaning which terms such as "history" and "historian" possess in statements like the following: "Mark was not

seeking to write history and is not an historian. His purpose was simpler. He wanted to tell how the Good News concerning Jesus Christ, God's Son began" (V. Taylor, *The Gospel According to St Mark* [London, 1955] p. 130). Léon-Dufour has accurately expressed the positive and negative connotations of such assertions in the following description of the practice of the Synoptic Evangelists: "Certes ils l'interprètent (le fait), ils le voient selon une optique, qui est celle de la foi. Et cependant la simplicité de la narration et des manières de parler, les difficultés qui découlent d'une telle naïveté dans la présentation doctrinale, l'union indissoluble de la doctrine et du fait qui rend impossible l'adhésion purement intellectuelle à l'Evangile mais requiert la reconnaissance du caractère divin de Jésus, tout cela converge pour montrer que les évangiles ne sont *pas une spéculation doctrinale, mais l'attestation d'un fait*" (*op cit.*, p. 329; the emphasis is Léon-Dufour's).

4. The preacher can measure the value he sets on precise historical statement by measuring his reaction to the following judgment of the nature of the Gospel accounts: "Often, when we look for the value of a particular passage, we may find that its primary value is other than historical" (J. L. McKenzie, in *Theological Studies* 21 [1960] 285). If he should feel that a passage of which the above might be justly said, e.g., the temptation story in Matthew and Luke, had for this reason lost much, if not all, value for him, he is gravely overvaluing the value of historical interest. Inasmuch as we are all tempted in this direction, we show in this the influence of our age.

5. The statement placed in the mouth of the preacher in the text is an exaggeration, although it has been heard once or twice. The number of Christians would be sharply reduced, if the scientific demonstration of the fact of Jesus from the Gospels were the only valid basis for the judgments of credibility and credentity. However, the preacher is correct in believing that this demonstration, though admittedly difficult, cannot be so exacting as to be practically impossible. Such hypercriticism, murmurs of which have sometimes been heard on the exegetical side of this modern Great Divide, would seem to run counter to the statements of the Vatican Council on the significance of "facta divina," and in particular of miracles and prophecies in the act of divine revelation (*DB* 1790, 1812-13).

6. Léon-Dufour (*op. cit.*, p. 322) summarizes the routine argument for the historicity of the Gospels and points up some of its lacunae. His entire chapter ("Les évangiles et l'histoire") offers the replacement which we imagine the preacher desiring. Other useful treatments of this are: C. H. Dodd, *History and the Gospel* (London, 1938), and E. Hoskyns and N. Davey, *The Riddle of the New Testament* (3rd ed., London, 1947).

7. W. F. Albright, *From the Stone Age to Christianity* (2nd ed.; Baltimore, 1946) pp. 48-49.

8. A. Schweitzer has given memorable expression to the spirit in which this quest was first undertaken: "Das Dogma musste erst erschüttert werden, ehe man den historischen Jesus wieder suchen, ehe man überhaupt den Gedanken sein Existenz fassen konnte. Dass er etwas anderes ist als der Jesus-Christus der Zweinaturenlehre, scheint uns heute etwas Selbstverständliches" (*Von Reimarus zu Wrede* [Tübingen, 1906] p. 3).

9. *Op. cit.*, p. 49.

10. "Jesus, St John and St Paul," in *The Root of the Vine* (New York, 1953) pp. 53-54.

11. *Ibid.*, p. 54.

12. Fridrichsen describes the results of this division of labor: the first century providing a historical kernel which should be interpreted by the nineteenth: "The application of this method in research concerning Jesus led inevitably to preposterous results. A picture of Jesus was drawn which was simply the idealized self-portrait of man in the nineteenth century" (*art. cit.*, pp. 54-55). Despite this bias, these years of investigation gave scholars precious insights into the sources that lie behind the Synoptic tradition.

13. I.e., between 1863, when H. J. Holtzmann published his epoch-making commentary on the Synoptics, and 1901, when Wrede's *Messiasgeheimnis in den Evangelien* appeared. For a rounded picture of the merits and weaknesses of Holtzmann's achievement, cf. W. G. Kümmel, *Das Neue Testament: Geschichte der Erforschung seiner Probleme* (Freiburg-Munich, 1958) pp. 185-86.

14. These examples of "forms" are taken from G. Bornkamm's recent excellent classification of the Synoptic material, "Formen und Gattungen II. Im NT," *Die Religion in Geschichte und Gegenwart* 2 (3rd ed.; Tübingen, 1958) 1000-1001.

15. E.g., careful study of their form has convinced Bornkamm that the Jesus-stories mentioned in the text were told "[um] Glauben und Erkenntnis zu wecken," whereas the Christus-stories were narrative expressions of Christian faith. "[Sie] sind . . . von vornherein und im ganzen von diesem Glauben geprägt." Similar investigation has shown that all the elements in the Synoptic tradition presuppose this faith and present their narratives from that viewpoint.

16. Cf. the discussion of the *Kerygma-Theologie* in N. A. Dahl, "Der historische Jesus als geschichtswissenschaftliches und theologisches Problem," *Kerygma und Dogma* 1 (1955) 112-113.

17. *Art. cit.*, pp. 55-56.

18. Cf. J. M. Robinson, *A New Quest of the Historical Jesus* (Naper-ville-London, 1959). Conservative scholars have tended to avoid the term "the historical Jesus" because of the distinction which those who coined it erected between it and the "Christ of faith." It is doubtful if we can do without some such term in the present discussion. Dahl (*art. cit.*, p. 104) has redefined it as follows: "[The term 'the historical Jesus'] denotes Jesus, inasmuch as He is the object of methodical, critical, historical investigation, and the pic-ture of Him which can be drawn as the result of such study." By transferring the concept from the ontological to the epistemo-logical realm, Dahl avoids the implications which had rendered the term unacceptable to traditional Christians. It is used in this sense in the present paper. Cf. also on this "new quest" J. Jeremias, "The Present Position of the Controversy concerning the Problem of the Historical Jesus," *ET* 69 (1958) 333-339, and P. Althaus, "Der gegenwärtige Stand der Frage nach dem historischen Jesus," *Sitz-berichte der Bayerischen Akademie der Wissenschaften, Phil.-hist. Klasse* (Munich, 1960).

19. Cf. Léon-Dufour, *op. cit.*, pp. 323-331, for a brief but clear outline of a modern demonstration of the historical worth of the Gospels.

20. R. Schnackenburg, *Gottes Herrschaft und Reich* (Freiburg, 1959) pp. 49-76. We might also add (with S., pp. 77-88) that the re-mainder of Jesus' salvific activity was intended by Him to be a sign of the proleptic presence of the Rule of God.

21. It may be useful to emphasize the nature of the assent which the historian gives to these hypotheses. As the Greek root suggests, these supply a foundation or basis for the investigation to be undertaken. The German term *Vorverständnis*, "preunderstand-ing," specifies the nature of this foundation. These hypotheses are composed of a series of prejudgments which express the best solutions which the previous study of the historian has uncovered for the various problems of the Gospel texts. Inasmuch as they are judgments, these solutions are firmly held, because a great number of individual texts converge to support them. Inasmuch as they are *pre*judgments, which have been made antecedently to and independently of the detailed analysis of the text under investiga-tion (in the present instance, the parable of the Sower), these solutions are considered to be highly probable but not definitive. They have enough support in the Gospel texts to provide a reasonable starting point for serious investigation. However, the historian is ready to modify them, or to abandon them in part or *in toto*, if further study of his texts imposes either of these de-cisions on him. This is the well known "heuristic circle" which is typical of the *Geisteswissenschaften* and must not be confused with the illegitimate logical circle. Here the argumentation is not linear as in logic, but all conclusions arrived at are a result of a convergence of individual facts. The heuristic circle here is a

means for establishing this convergence. Cf. also the stimulating articles of Bultmann on this point: "Ist voraussetzungslose Exegese möglich?" *TZ* (Basel) 13 (1957) 409-417 (incorporated in *Glauben und Verstehen* 3 [Tübingen, 1960]), and "Wissenschaft und Existenz," in *Ehrfurcht vor dem Leben* (*Festschrift A. Schweitzer,* 1955); also in *Glauben und Verstehen* 3, 107-121).

22. The writer is particularly indebted to the following studies of Mark 4:1-9, 13-20 and parallels (the names in brackets indicate how these works will be cited in future notes): N. A. Dahl, "The Parables of Growth," *Studia theologica* 5 (1952) 132-166 [Dahl II]; J. Jeremias, *Die Gleichnisse Jesu* (2nd ed.; Zurich, 1952) [Jeremias]; J. Schmid, *Das Evangelium nach Markus* (4th ed.; Regensburg, 1958) [Schmid]; R. Schnackenburg, "Die Lehre der Wachstumsgleichnisse," in *Gottes Herrschaft und Reich* (Freiburg, 1959) pp. 98-109 [Schnackenburg]; V. Taylor, *The Gospel according to St. Mark* (London, 1955) [Taylor].

23. This is true of Matthew and Mark. Luke reproduces the Marcan complex in his parallel chapter 8 only as far as the interpretation of the Sower.

24. So Jeremias, p. 99; Dahl II, pp. 146, 147-152 *passim.*

25. Dahl II. p. 147, n. 2, cites as evidence here: Dan. 4:11, 18 (Theod. 4: 12, 21), Ezek. 31:6, Judg. 9:15, Lam. 4:20, 1 Bar. 1:12.

26. Schnackenburg, p. 106, follows Jeremias, p. 96, in relating the abnormally large mass of dough in the parable of the Leaven to the plenitude of the *Gottesherrschaft.*

27. Dahl II, p. 146, interprets the phenomenon of growth in these parables as follows: "To the growth which God in accordance with his own established order gives in the sphere of organic life, corresponds the series of events by which God in accordance with his plan of salvation leads history towards the end of the world and the beginning of the new aeon. This should, however, not be taken to mean that we must seek the point of the parables in this idea of growth. Rather, it is presupposed as a matter of course."

28. Dahl II, p. 148.

29. Dahl II, p. 153 cites as *OT* witness for the note of exceptional fertility in the Messianic Age: Amos 9:13, Jl 2:19 ff. and 4:18, Is. 4:2, Jer. 31:12, Ez. 34:27 and 36:29 f. This notion took on quite fantastic proportions in later Jewish literature.

30. Jeremias, p. 18.

31. Taylor, p. 254. For details cf. Taylor *in loco* and Jeremias, pp. 60-61.

32. Schmid, p. 93.

33. Schnackenburg, p. 103: "Dazu erklärt Jesus: Dennoch ist der Anfang gemacht, und das kommende Reich naht unaufhaltsam. . . . Gott führt sein Werk auch unter diesen Umständen zu Ende."

34. For this interpretation and its *Sitz im Leben Jesu,* cf. Schnackenburg, p. 103.

35. Schmid, p. 97.

36. *Ibid.*

37. Taylor, p. 261: "But the climax is not emphasized and developed; the earlier stages have absorbed the commentator's attention. All therefore that he has to say is that the people in question hear the word, welcome it. . . . They are a mere foil to the discreditable types." As will be seen later, however, we disagree heartily with Taylor's conclusion from these observations: "So little is the parable understood!"

38. Jeremias, pp. 40-41.

39. Despite the new emphasis on the activity of the Evangelists in the work of the *Redaktionsgeschichtliche Schule,* Wikenhauser's judgment on the Synoptic Gospels remains true: "die syn Evv sind Sammelwerke" (*Einleitung in das NT* [2nd ed.; Freiburg, 1956] p. 196). Although new evidence has been brought to light to demonstrate the theological interest of these men, the literary activity which expressed this interest was "editorial" rather than "compositional."

40. Cf. reference in n. 2.

41. The reader should not imagine that the historian proposes this solution without careful consideration of the alternatives. Jeremias, p. 60, has expressed his reluctance as follows: "Ich habe mich lange gegen den Schluss gesträubt, dass diese Gleichnisdeutung der Urkirche zugeschrieben werden muss." The distinction in strata is imposed by the fact that no other hypothesis will reasonably account for the congeries of phenomena which have to be explained: differences in vocabulary and language, difference in problems faced, the employment of allegorization, together with the fact that these phenomena recur in other passages which present further evidence of belonging to a later stratum. The stratum, however, is not very late. The absence of any Marcan peculiarities leads most scholars to date this material before Mark, i.e., before *ca.* 65 A.D.

42. Mark 4:10-12 par. Taylor, p. 254, judges this pericope to be a Markan construction" on the basis of received tradition.

43. Dahl II, p. 158.

44. This is particularly true of Mark 4:17b-19; cf. Taylor, p. 261.

45. Schnackenburg, p. 104.

46. Jeremias, p. 33. These words were written in commentary on Luke 16: 8-13, which contains a series of applications appended to the parable of the Unjust Steward.

47. Mark 4:21-22; cf. Schmid, p. 101.

48. The limits referred to above exclude any statement which would disrupt the essential conformity which must exist between the past event and its historical record. The nature of the Gospels forces us to expect this from the Evangelists. The problem here, however, is: Does the adaptation of Jesus' words to another audience destroy this essential conformity? Fridrichsen answers in the negative (*art. cit.*, p. 39) and explains how this is so: "Jesus' teaching, His Sermon on the Mount, and His parables belong to His activity among God's people of old times, *in the last days of the ancient era.* Formally and objectively they bear the stamp of that activity, and of its special purpose in preparing the congregation of the Jewish Synagogue for the Kingdom of God. *But, at the same time, they bear the new age within them.* Therefore it has been possible for them to be adapted by the Church, and in the light of the Resurrection, and the fellowship of the Spirit, to become the Word of the Lord to His redeemed people" (emphasis added). Therefore, by adapting Jesus' words to her children, the Early Church not only fulfilled a practical, apostolic purpose. By this very procedure she reflected an aspect of the historical actuality of Jesus of Nazareth which would have been overlooked, had she merely reproduced His words exactly as He had spoken them.

49. The mentality of the Evangelists has rarely been better described than in these words of Fridrichsen (*art. cit.*, p. 43): "Faith builds upon history and includes it, but associates it with the present, and aspires to the future consummation." The idea is not new. Thomas Aquinas was driven to join the same ideas together in pondering the evangelical accounts of the Last Supper: cf. "O sacrum convivium."

50. One excellent way by which the English-speaking preacher can keep in contact with exegetical work is to consult regularly *New Testament Abstracts,* published at Weston College, Weston, Mass.

51. As seems clear from the counsel of the Holy Father that other Christians should judge the work of exegetes not only "aequo justoque animo," but also "summa caritate" (*EB* 564).

P. De Letter

>>>>><<<<<

THE ENCOUNTER
WITH GOD

PRESENT-DAY personalistic trends in the theology of grace, of faith and of the sacraments manifest a preference for the expression "meeting God" or "meeting Christ." The idea of an encounter with God seems to be a key concept. And it obviously reflects a desire for genuineness and depth in living by one's religion. Yet, one may well ask, for how many who use the phrase is it more than a catchword for the imagination or for the evocation of an ill-defined religious sentiment? We do not mean to suggest that the idea does not express, in the minds of

177

the theologians who coined and popularized the phrase, a great, if mysterious, reality. It has, moreover, a precedent in the name which the Greek liturgy gives to the feast of Our Lord's presentation in the temple, *hypapante tou theou* (Simon's) meeting with God. When theologians speak of religion as a dialogue between God and man, placing its deepest experience in man's encounter with God, they undoubtedly know what they mean to say, wishing to present the inner mystery of the Christian life in a way appealing to the modern mind and heart.

The idea of an encounter with God is central in a theology which conceives the life of grace as a complex of relationships, in the first place with Christ and the Triune God.[1] It is basic in a personalistic theology of faith, which sees in faith first and foremost an enlightened and trustful surrender to a Person: I believe in Thee.[2] It is one of the hinges of a theology of the sacraments conceived as "actions of Christ," actions of the glorious Christ present and active in the grace-giving rites of the Church, His mystical Body.[3] The setting of this idea of an encounter with God shows its importance in our contemporary approach to the study of God, an approach which centers in man more than in God. It is mainly from the angle of our relationships with Him as Creator, Redeemer, Sanctifier, that the Triune God "interests" our contemporaries and contemporary theology. Revelation, they insist, is in the first place a history of salvation, and theology is the study of God as author of our salvation. This approach, moreover, is quite legitimate. The Christian message, the object of revelation and of theology, is not a mere supernatural metaphysics, but a doctrine of salvation. And in this message and doctrine the idea of an encounter with God holds a necessary place.

That being the case, it should be rewarding to try and have, as far as we can, a definite and firm grasp of its meaning. What does the idea of an encounter with God convey both ontologically and psychologically? Though directly expressing a psychological happening, namely, a meeting of persons, this very event is an ontological reality, and one in which supernatural factors play a role. This is precisely the intriguing aspect of the whole concept: what does a supernatural encounter with God mean whether in man's awareness or in objective reality?

The supernatural, in fact, is not as such the immediate object of awareness: we know of it only through faith and further from signs and situations or from facts which allow us to conjecture or deduce the presence of what faith teaches. A "living" faith may give some sort of intuition of the mysterious reality, and this is no doubt what is suggested by the idea of an encounter with God: it means to say that there is not only an "ontological contact" with God, but there is some "experience" of that contact. This makes it all the more intriguing, and urgently invites an analysis of its objective or ontological and subjective or psychological contents. What does the encounter with God in grace, faith and the sacraments involve by way of ontological reality? To what extent and in what manner does this reality appear in our awareness? These are the two questions that must be answered if we wish to catch a glimpse of the mysterious happening.

THE THEOLOGY OF ENCOUNTER

If we may take it that a meeting of persons is essentially the I-Thou relationship, such as we know it from direct experience in our human relations with our fellow men,[4] then it appears at once that it means union in distinction or opposition: it is a union with another as other or as distinct and opposed. Such a relationship is necessarily of the intentional order, that is, on the level of knowledge and love. To know and to love means a relation to another as other, a union without fusion, a union which is a psychological fact of experience. A psychological fact, however, in sound philosophy, supposes an objective or ontological contact, inasmuch as awareness is in fact only the consciousness of both self and its relationships with other persons or things. Persons therefore meet in mutual knowledge and love.

This is true also when the meeting happens to be between a human and a divine Person. The encounter with God, still less than contact with another human person, can never mean ontological fusion; an abyss separates Creator and creature. Consequently it cannot be other than an intentional union in which the human person and the divine Person(s) are united while remaining distinct and opposed. It is therefore in mutual knowledge and love that the encounter takes place. And since the encounter with God which we are studying belongs to the life of grace, of faith and of the sacraments, we know that this knowledge and love are of the order of grace, or supernatural. And so the theology of the encounter with God, in its objective and ontological reality, is to be looked for in the theology of grace, of faith and of the sacraments.

THE LIFE OF GRACE

The life of grace, both in traditional and contemporary theology, involves an ontological transformation of the soul in the state of grace, and as a condition and effect alike of this transformation, a new relationship to the indwelling Triune God. In other words, created grace, the inherent *habitus* of sanctifying grace, and Uncreated Grace or the divine indwelling are of necessity together: they are correlatives having between them the reciprocal priority and causality which plays between coexisting components of any one complex reality. This relationship to the Triune God, according to an ever more widely accepted view of theology today,[5] unites to the Three Persons as they are distinct from one another. It is a relationship which is threefold because of the Three Persons to whom the justified soul is both linked and opposed; yet both because of the oneness of nature in the Three Persons and of the unity of created sanctifying grace, its foundation, this relationship should be said to be triune rather than threefold.

This relationship is an ontological, objective reality: the relation of the soul to the indwelling Triune God is real because of the reality of created sanctifying grace; it exists independently of our actual knowing or willing. Yet, it belongs to the order of intentional union, that is, to the level of cognitional and volitional activity since its opposes while uniting; it does not play on the level of *esse* or being: there is in no way ontological fusion which would mean suppression of our personality. But it is an intentional union of a particular type, for it exists even in the absence of acts of knowledge and love on our part and results from the presence in the soul of the habitual principles of such acts, namely, of sanctifying grace and the infused virtues. That is what St. Thomas taught when explaining the divine indwelling which, he says, means the presence in the just of the divine Persons as object of knowledge and love by virtue of sanctifying grace and in the absence of particular acts of knowledge and love.[6] The intentional union with the divine Persons through grace does not, therefore, of necessity involve an actual psychological awareness, since it exists without such acts. What it then means on the psychological level we shall have to explain later. At this point we can only say that the encounter with God involved in the life of grace is an onological contact between the human person in the state of grace and the divine Persons. The very reality of sanctifying grace as the foundation of the divine indwelling or of the relationship of union with the divine Persons implies this contact.

THE LIFE OF FAITH

A similar contact is involved in the particular manifestation of the life of grace which is faith. The personalistic approach to the theology of faith, as proposed, for example, by J. Mouroux,[7] rests indeed on a firm theological basis. This is to be found not only nor chiefly in the conceptual expression of faith in which we confess that we believe in God, accepting as true, on the authority of His testimony guaranteed by the Church, whatever truth He has revealed.

This confession of faith, to be sure, is neither meaningful nor genuine unless it can be the expression of a trusting personal surrender to the Uncreated Truth, that is, of a personal attitude of loving trust toward the Triune God. This attitude, however, is only partially expressed in the formulated act of faith; it involves a deeper-lying reality. Why? Because faith is not possible without grace, without a supernatural gift; it is supernatural knowledge born and permeated by the grace or light of faith. But this light of faith is no matter of conceptual formulation. As every grace, it is an ontological reality in man's soul, in this case in his mind, and secondarily also in the will, a reality which is the foundation and reason of a real relation of union with the Uncreated Grace, here, the Uncreated Truth.

Accordingly, there is in faith, an, as it were, more external or extrinsic psychological aspect, namely, the conceptual expression of our faith in God, and a deeper and hidden ontological contact with the Triune God as Uncreated Truth.[8] This contact, like every union of grace, is of the intentional order or of the level of cognition, yet it does not as such directly and clearly appear in our awareness. The encounter with God in faith takes place, just as that of the divine indwelling by grace, even in the absence of definite acts of faith. The grace or light of faith, as we know, is not a passing actual grace but a permanent habitual gift. As long as this gift exists in the mind, man's supernatural union with the Uncreated Truth also continues, since the grace of faith is of its essence a link with the supreme Truth.

The contact or encounter with the Triune God in faith is not, therefore, in the first place a matter of conceptual knowledge and conceptual awareness; for this awareness flowers only on the foundation of a supernatural union through the grace of faith. The grace or light of faith, as a real and objective link of the mind with the Uncreated Truth, constitutes the ontology of the encounter with God in faith. And as in the case of the divine indwelling by grace, so also in particular for faith, we shall have to examine how and to what extent this ontological encounter with the Triune God reveals itself in the consciousness, if indeed it does.

THE SACRAMENTS

A third case of meeting God, this time in the definite shape of a meeting with Christ, is found in the theology of the sacraments. We may refer here in particular to the profound and inspiring sacramental theology proposed in recent years by Fr. H. Schillebeeckx, O.P.[9] The sacraments are actions of the gloriously living Christ who, through the medium of sensible signs of spiritual grace, of which the Church is the depository and administrator, continues His work of redemption by dispensing the graces of salvation. He gained for us by His life, death and resurrection. Christ's action in the sacraments is hidden, and only faith enables us to detect it. It is, however, the very core and heart of the "sacramental economy of salvation" such as it is proposed and effectuated in the teaching and action of the Church. It is Christ coming to meet us, and in Him, through the instrumentality of His glorious humanity, the Father and the Holy Spirit: the Triune God.

An encounter, however, is no meeting of persons if it is

unilateral. To be a personal meeting, it supposes a move on the part of both persons who come together. In fact, the Church's doctrine on the sacraments holds, and contemporary sacramental theology is fond of emphasizing this aspect of her teaching, that our cooperation is necessary for the fruitful reception of the sacraments, that is, to allow Christ's action to be effective. Unless we bring to the sacraments the right dispositions, Christ's action has no effect; and the quality of our dispositions in a way measures the degree of its fruitfulness.[10] This teaching only applies to the case of sacramental sanctification what the Council of Trent taught and theology teaches today about the subjective dispositions necessary for the reception and increase of grace.[11] Grace is not obtruded on the unwilling; our free acceptance is indispensable and gives the measure of our enrichment, no less in the sacraments than outside. In terms of a personalistic theology: to the action of Christ coming to meet us in the sacraments must correspond on our part our own going to meet Him, by our desire and readiness or proper dispositions to accept His grace. The reception of a sacrament, therefore, is an encounter with God, a meeting with the God-man and in Him with the Triune God.

Such an encounter, evidently, is in the first place an ontological event, a happening that takes place on the level of the supernatural reality of grace which, we said already, does not lie within the field of our immediate awareness. That it does take place, in the very joining of Christ's action dispensing grace and our free acceptance of His gift, the teaching of the faith guarantees; and human observation allows us sufficient insight to be certain, with the certainty we can have of human events, of the valid reception of the sacraments. The two combined, faith and observation, allow also a certainty of the mysterious event, the divine encounter.[12] Whether and how far we can have any other awareness of this event besides this indirect knowledge, we shall have to consider presently.

Thus far the theology of the encounter with God implied in the current theology of grace, of faith and of the sacraments. It teaches beyond a shadow of doubt that an ontological meeting between the human person and the divine Persons takes place in the life of grace, in faith and in the sacraments. The teaching of the faith and common theology vouch for it.

THE PSYCHOLOGY OF ENCOUNTER

It is apparently the psychology of the encounter with God that requires closer investigation. A meeting of persons, we have hinted already, is of necessity a psychological event. We know who he is we are meeting. And it entails a direct knowledge of the person we meet, not only that obtained from secondhand information. If the idea of an encounter with God has any meaning, we must know who He is we are meeting, and apparently know this by some sort of direct knowledge. We have then to ask: What idea of the Person of Christ or of the divine Persons of the Holy Trinity is necessary for the experience of the divine encounter? And is there also a direct knowledge of the Triune God whom we meet in grace, in faith and the sacraments?

The question may not be easy; a fully satisfactory

answer is hardly possible, because we touch here on the mysterious realities which surpass our human understanding. The answer may not be limited to the case of mystical experience, of the experience of grace, which, if not exceptional, at any rate is not common, granted by special divine favor to those endowed with infused contemplation. The mystical experience may throw light on the mystery, especially if we hold, with the more common opinion of today's spiritual theology, that it is nothing else than the privileged direct experience of the supernatural reality which is present in every soul in the state of grace.[13] The psychology of the encounter with God must fit also the common Christian experience.[14] The life of grace is such an encounter in every Christian who lives by grace. Its awareness may differ in degree of vividness; in some or many it may be dimmed by distraction or engrossment in external or temporal pursuits. But it ought to be there in some degree; else one cannot see how there is any sense in saying that a meeting with the Triune God is the heart of the life of grace.

MEETING A PERSON

The knowledge of a person, such as is involved in and necessary for meeting a person, is not a purely conceptual knowledge.[15] Even apart from direct contact, the idea we form of someone, from past experiences or from an indirect knowledge of his actions, sayings or writings, is not a mere concept or synthesis of concepts; it is rather a sort of general synthetic intuition resulting, not by reasoning but by "seeing," from the assemblage of many partial experiences or ideas. It apparently cannot be anything else if it is to be knowledge of the person, of the someone, of the *who* he is, and not merely of *what* he is. The knowledge of a person cannot be expressed in a concept which of its nature reifies a quality or form or idea and does not of itself represent a subject, a *suppositum*, a *who*. No doubt, some conceptual knowledge, some imaginative or sensible description, a composite of partial images or impressions, is necessary as an attendant picture of the person but the pure "subject" or *who* cannot be conceived. Nor does a concept express the individuality of the person. But the picture we make of someone is secondary, it may be more or less full, it may be imperfect without affecting our knowledge of the person. This knowledge is rather a sort of intuition in which the mind's eye shifts from the "whatness" or "quiddity" to the "whoness" or personality, an intuition best expressed in the suggestive I-Thou relationship.

In fact, the very idea of person, in today's personalistic trends of thought, involves relation and opposition to other persons.[16] The traditional scholastic notion insisting on the self-containedness of the individual in a rational nature is incomplete and one-sided, and should be completed with that of relative opposition to other persons. The idea of relation, it is said today, enters the very notion of person. This view is shared by thinkers who have no inkling of the transcendent manner in which it is verified within the Blessed Trinity, where the Persons are subsistent relations. The I of the person of its nature calls for the Thou of the I-Thou relation. Rather it is mainly by its relative opposition to the Thou of another that the I of the subject comes to realize his self-awareness as a person.

If this view of personality is acceptable—and there is no reason to say that it is not, if only we keep the core of truth of the ancient idea of person and do not reduce the person to a mere relation without "absolute" reality— then it appears at once how real knowledge of a person cannot be purely conceptual but must be intuitive in some way. Only by intuition do we really know a relation, not by conceptual knowledge: a relation is not something (and all concepts represent something), not a *quid* or *esse*, but a "toward something," an *ad quid*, an *esse ad*. Some knowledge of the *quid* must go with it, no doubt; but as said already, this may be incomplete and give an imperfect picture of the person's qualities. The intuition which reaches the person himself comes rather from the light of the synthetic view, the *lumen* which gradually dawns or suddenly springs on us; we express it in the nonconceptual *he* or *You* (subject, not object), as when we say of someone's doing "that is," or address him as "you."

What, then, meeting a person involves by way of psychological or intentional contact should be clear from the above. Meeting a person is essentially the conscious living of the I-Thou relationship which, in mutual knowledge and love, unites and opposes two persons.[17] It supposes some conceptual knowledge of the person we meet, but it is not this knowledge which constitutes the personal contact. The contact lies rather in the direct knowledge of him; among human persons this knowledge is in the first place a sense perception or sense intuition, but it is more than that; it is the knowledge by which we attain the *who*, rather than the *what*, the who meaning the subject or someone who synthesizes in himself all the qualities or descriptions we may happen to know of him, but which are in a way distinct from him. He is the hearth, the center, the core and substratum of the qualities, the mysterious and literally ineffable and inexpressible Thou whom we understand by contrast and opposition with our own I. In this global intuition, knowledge and love combine in one experience, enriching us by making us live up to our reality as persons related to other persons. When we reflect on our past experience, we may come to realize that meeting a person, in a fully human encounter of direct knowledge of love, is in fact an enriching and in each case a unique experience.

THE MEETING WITH CHRIST

A similar experience, it would seem, is experienced in our meeting with Christ and with the Triune God of our Christian revelation which faith and theology allow us to expect in the life of grace or faith or in the reception of the sacraments. We said, similar; we should rather say, analogous, that is, partly similar and partly different. For there is here an additional mysterious factor which enters the experience, namely, supernatural grace with its immediate contact with the Infinite. The ineffableness proper even to each created person is enhanced infinitely in the case of the divine Persons.[18] Yet, the teaching of faith and theology is an invitation to try and "realize" the personal contact with the Triune God. Even a partially successful attempt should prove enriching. When attempting here to get some glimpse of the encounter with God, we may overlook the particularities which may differentiate that of the life of grace or of faith from the encounter which takes place in the reception of the sacraments. We shall mainly try to analyze first our meeting with Christ, and then our meeting with the Triune God, the Persons of the Blessed Trinity.

The psychology of the encounter with Christ involved particularly in the reception of the sacraments, and also, if less explicitly, in the life of grace and of faith, must, in keeping with the psychology of meeting a person, be said to be made of a twofold strand. There is first the mental picture of Christ, or the conceptual representation each one makes of Him for himself of what He was and continues to be; this picture sums up, perhaps in an unclear manner, what we know about Him: about His human and divine nature, His divine Person, His human life and life work on earth, His glorious life now. It synthesizes our knowledge of *what* He is, rather than of *who* He is. Besides this, and more important is the direct knowledge of Him glimpsed in the sacramental contact through the "intuition" of faith. A closer study of both these elements should reveal as far as it can the inner psychology of the encounter with Christ.

THE MENTAL PICTURE OF CHRIST

It is a fact to which every Christian with some inner life can testify that each one of us carries with himself a mental representation of Christ, the God-man, our Redeemer, which is a representation all his own.[19] Though none of us in the twentieth century have ever seen Christ with the eyes of his body, neither as He was seen by the people of Palestine when He lived on earth, nor as He is now in the glory of His Father, yet each one constructs for himself his own mental picture of Christ, more or less full, more or less definite, more or less permanent though evolving with time and age. It is the result of all that we have learned about Him and assimilated and made our own, in study and prayer, in reading or in contemplation of Christian art, or in mental prayer. This image of Christ varies from man to man, yet it is substantially the same in all its countless variations. Its chief features, which constitute as it were its intellectual framework and main outline, are the doctrinal ideas which we draw from our faith and revelation. Christ is the God-man, the Word Incarnate, the Second Person of the Trinity who was made flesh for our salvation, true God and true man, who lived and died for us and rose again from the dead. This dogmatic description of Christ, for all its basic importance, is rather vague and jejune as a mental or imaginative picture; there are no or few individual features, and those there are may be of doubtful origin. The picture needs to be filled in with concrete and living detail; and here is the place of our study and meditation on the gospel. For this purpose prayer more than study is apt to make the picture come to life. In fact, experience of the spiritual life attests, it is mainly by a life of prayer that we come to detect Christ as a living person, who is concerned about us and plays a role now in our very lives.

It should be noted here that the decisive element in our mental picture of Christ is less that of any of the particular features that go into its making and are generally rather blurred and dimmed than that of their synthesizing principle. And this is more a matter of love than of knowledge. Even in our human relationships we form for ourselves mental pictures of the persons we know and love well, pictures in which the photographic outline and detail may be dim and ill defined, varying with time and changing circumstances, and which yet convey the image of very definite and living personalities. And it is more our love and affection than the sense images or the various features of the mental image which breathe life into the picture. So also, on the higher plane of religion, our representation of Christ is in the last instance determined by our love for Him. Love, it is said, give eyes to see. It transfigures and vivifies what otherwise might have been a lifeless image or a dead souvenir. And this all the more so as the human features of our picture of Christ, however exalted and sublime they may be, of necessity fall short of the reality. They can never convey the full idea of the God-man, they stop at the representation of the man. No conceptual representation is by itself an adequate means to express the true personality of Christ, His divine Person. It is therefore by another way, that of love, that we are to arrive at a personal contact with Christ. Love is the way to a living encounter with Christ.

DIRECT "INTUITION"

It is through faith, we said above, that we come to know of Christ's action in the sacraments. This faith, especially when enlivened by love, as for clarity and briefness' sake we may suppose it does, implies an existential judgment and an existential or personal attitude, and this includes some sort of direct intuition of the Person of Christ who initiates the dialogue of our sanctification by His sacramental action. The analysis of this intuitive side of faith[20] and love should unfold to our eyes, as far as is possible, the mysterious encounter with Christ in its psychological vitality.

The faith by which we come into personal contact with Christ sanctifying us in the sacraments is not only an intellectual assent to a conceptually formulated truth, to a statement whether of principle or of fact. The conceptual expression of what we believe is only one aspect of the faith, and the more extrinsic at that. There is also the affirmation, the saying Yes, apparently to an inevident truth, in fact to a Person.[21] For the assent of faith is dependent on or commanded by the will (only they believe who wish to believe), and both mind and will are supernaturalized by the grace of faith and love. This free assent goes in the first place to the Person in whose testimony and authority we believe and who guarantees the truth of what we accept as true. It is first of all a surrender of loving trust to the subsistent Truth who is a Person, and only in the second place the Yes to a particular point of faith. In this surrender which includes the whole human person, mind and will, knowledge and affectivity, the mental picture we have of Christ is a necessary condition but an inadequate expression of the Person. The surrender of faith goes beyond the picture to the Person Himself glimpsed in a sort of dark and formless intuition of loving faith.

Actually when we receive the sacraments in "a spirit of faith," that is, being aware of what we are doing, we have a knowledge of Christ's sanctifying action not only by a theoretical reasoning based on the teaching of revelation and on self-observation, but also in the existential answer we give to His initiative in the dialogue of the life of grace. Our loving surrender to Him or our free co-operation with His sacramental action is borne by and realizes a dark but true sense of His presence, a dark but effective intuition of His Person. We do not surrender blindly, no, we know what we are doing and what is happening, from the light of all that faith teaches about Christ and His sacramental action. But we surrender, mind and will, more to the attraction of love than to the light of knowledge, at any rate of clear and conceptual knowledge.[22] There is here an actual encounter with Christ, a meeting with Him as of two persons, in the very reception of the sacraments. Our realization of it depends on the attention we pay to the supernatural event which takes place in the depth of our souls, hidden under the sacramental appearances.

This intuition of Christ is no new clarity on the level of conceptual knowledge, in particular it is no new clarity of our mental picture of Christ as to its outline and features. It is a new clarity or a new knowledge of the Person of Christ, in the sense of a new intentional union or union of loving knowledge, or of knowledge by connaturality. This union takes place in the dimness of faith inherent in our state as pilgrims. It means a personal knowledge and love of Christ which, in its psychology, is not unlike the concrete knowledge of a human person that we gain in actual intercourse. Even in human intercourse the hard core of the person, so to speak, remains a sealed mystery. Our conceptual and sensible knowledge of man does not touch this. Only love can give a deeper insight into the *who* of the person. A similar insight or intuition attends the supernatural event which consists in the meeting of our *opus operantis* and Christ's *opus operatum* in the reception of a sacrament. The growth in the life of grace consequent on that reception means a deeper knowledge and attachment to Christ. We do not learn new things in the sense of an enrichment of our conceptual knowledge of Him, but we do learn to know better *who* He is; He comes to mean to us more than He did before, our love of Him grows and makes Him more real to us than He was before.

What does this deeper insight, this sort of intuition of the Person of Christ actually mean? The analogy with our direct knowledge of human persons may help us to understand. Just as the deeper knowledge of a human person which results from personal intercourse leads us to discover in him "someone" on whom we can rely, that is, the core of his personality, the subject or support of all the qualities and accidental or external features, often enough without adding to our "pictorial" knowledge of him or of *what* he is: so also the encounter with Christ allows us to realize ever better who He is on whom we can count without danger or fear of disappointment. In Him we discover, not a human person who might prove unreliable, but the absolutely reliable divine Person. It is the intuition of loving faith which attains the transcendent core of the divine personality of Christ. And this discovery is the answer to what is most central in the religious aspirations: the need of an absolute on which we can rest both our weakness as creatures and our aspirations for the infinite, without any possibility of His giving way or disappointing our trust.

The liturgy and the psalms often express the jubilant joy of this discovery; the Lord God is my refuge and my strength, my savior and redeemer! This is the immovable Rock we reach by the intuition and surrender of loving faith in the encounter with Christ. This, then, it appears, is the psychology of our meeting with the divine Person in Christ, as He comes to meet us in His sacramental action.

MEETING THE TRIUNE GOD

In Christ we also meet the Holy Trinity. He is for us the entrance door to the sharing in the Trinitarian life which is the life of grace. Contemporary theology is more and more inclined to emphasize the Trinitarian aspect of the supernatural life. In contrast with the order of nature or of creation which relates us to God as one, the order of grace and of our re-creation brings us in contact with the Triune God.[23] Moreover, if the life of grace in its essence is a personal encounter with God who is a Trinity of Persons, it cannot but involve a triune relationship with the divine Persons.

The psychology or experiential living of this Trinitarian relationship comprises the same two elements that were just studied in our meeting with Christ. There is the mental representation of the Triune God, and there is the intuitional contact with the Three divine Persons. Each of these requires a further analysis.

CONCEPTUAL IMAGE OF THE TRIUNE GOD

However difficult may be the analysis of our conceptual image of the Triune God,[24] there can be no doubt about the necessity of such an image in the psychology of the life of grace. A psychological contact with the Triune God supposes some conceptual representation, however inadequate it may be. We cannot think or be aware of someone without shaping for ourselves some mental picture. The difficulty is increased in this case because, unlike Christ who is the God-man and whom we rightly represent as a man, the divine Persons cannot be represented to our minds except in an anthropomorphic way. We cannot but conceive of them after the analogy of human persons. This insinuates the extreme imperfection of our concept of the divine Persons, inadequate and incomplete, and in need all along of correction and sublimation.

There is no need to insist long on the imaginative element that enters our mental representation of the divine Persons: this evidently can have only a metaphorical value. No feature or form which is an object of the senses, exterior or interior, including the imagination, can apply properly to the divine Persons who are purely spiritual, and therefore can be nothing more than a metaphor. Because every one of our concepts, even the most abstract, of necessity involves some sensible image, however minimal it may be, in the case of our concepts of the divine Persons this image veils much more than it reveals their reality.

Even on their spiritual side, as intellectual representations, our concepts of the divine Persons must needs fall infinitely short of the reality they evoke. All our concepts are finite of their nature, they are limited forms of the objects they represent, even when these objects are infinite as in the case of the divine Persons. And we may well endeavor to remedy this inadequacy by opening out, at is were, the closed limitation of the concepts to a sort of indefiniteness to allow an unlimited perspective on the infinite they attempt to represent; nevertheless the representation is still altogether inadequate. The indefiniteness suggestive of infiniteness is a negative rather than a positive representation of the infinite.

Yet, despite this twofold inadequacy, both of the sensible picture and of the conceptual image, our mental representation of the Triune God has a positive content.[25] The concept of person, when applied to God, purified of its imperfections and limitations, conveys the idea of a subsistent spiritual self-contained reality, the ontological core of an I. The infiniteness which we must predicate of the divine Persons is the transcendent fullness of being which is beyond our conception. The Trinity of Persons within the one divinity also expresses an objective reality: Father, Son and Holy Spirit are distinct from one another, while subsisting in the one divine nature, by their mutual relative opposition.[26] Nor does the synthesis of oneness in nature and Trinity in Persons, expressed in their Triunity, involve any contradictory element, because unity and trinity deal with distinct aspects of the divine reality; essence and personality, *What* and *Who* respectively.[27] All this is but the conceptual expression of the Church's teaching concerning the mystery of the Blessed Trinity.

But does it not look like a playing with concepts, the play of a juggler who skillfully avoids every false step of contradiction but fails to reveal the secret of the elusive divine Triunity? Something more than this conceptual image of the Triune God is needed for a psychological encounter with the divine Persons.

THE INTUITIVE APPROACH

It is by way of faith and love in their unitive aspect as surrender from person to Person that the encounter with the divine Persons leads to the new discovery of their personality which constitutes a spiritual enrichment akin to and by far surpassing the gain involved in every intimate meeting of persons. Loving faith, we said already, gives new eyes and a new insight into the mystery of personality, as it does into the unfathomable mystery of the Three Persons in one God. Its new light somehow pierces or plunges into the twofold mystery of the Triunity, that of each of the divine Persons, and that of their unity in diversity.

There is first a new understanding of the divine Persons in their distinction and personality.[28] In this intuitive approach Father, Son and Holy Spirit, who take the initative in the dialogue of grace, reveal themselves as the divine Persons who loved us first and enable us to return Their love. This is no more than a glimpse of Their infinite reliability. But in this glimpse each of the Three appears, each in His own manner of existence within the Trinity; the Father as the answer to our need for strength and support; the Son for light and understanding; the Holy Spirit for love and enthusiasm. The Father is the One on whose all-powerful, changeless strength we can rest our creaturely dependence without afterthought, His omnipotence being the ready and watchful helpfulness of a Father. The Son, firstborn among many brothers, is He in whom the image and wisdom of the Father shines in full brightness and fills beyond measure our desire for knowing the Father "by connaturality," by being remade more and more in the image of the Son. The Holy Spirit is He who is the love of the Father and the Son and who carries us along in the powerful stream of love that springs from the inner life of the divine mystery and leads back to the same unsoundable depths.

This discovery of Father, Son and Holy Spirit does not spring from a reasoning reflection on what faith and theology teach us about them. That reflection may and must have preceded such reflection, in varying measure of depth and penetration, which is different for different persons. But all this conceptual knowledge is as it were condensed and swallowed up in the three *whos*, the three mysterious someones, who draw us by the current of grace and love to answer their initative with our surrender. In this very answer, despite the darkness or dimness of faith and love owing to the absence and neglect of conceptual clarity,[29] in this contact of mysterious knowledge and love the transcendent Three reveal themselves as the infinite divine Persons. We come to know, by the connaturality which grace gives, we sense, we learn from what we are living and experiencing, that They are the Rock on which we must build our trust and infinite aspiration. We feel we are safe in anchoring in Them our hope and our entire being: They are the changeless and immovable Three who are one infinite Love. Those among the faithful who live by their faith and love of the Triune God sense the fullness of meaning hidden in the names, Father, Son, and Holy Spirit. And though unable to express in words what is ineffable in each of the Three Persons, they realize beyond words and concepts who They are for each one of us.

Besides allowing us to realize in a sort of intuitive insight the distinction and proper characteristics of Father, Son and Holy Spirit, the eyes of loving faith lead to another discovery, that of the unity of the Persons or of their Triunity. It may be no easy task to formulate in concepts and words the mystery of their unity in distinction in such a manner so as not to leave the impression of solving a puzzle with a verbal distinction between relative and absolute reality in God. This is a solution which may satisfy the mind notionally but which may leave one unconvinced and without real understanding. But the insight of loving faith, in the surrender that answers the call of grace, grants those who believe and love a sense of the reality and rightness of the mystery. They "see" that it is so, without exactly seeing how and why. Christians who live by their faith know without sensing any difficulty that the three divine Persons are One God while being really distinct from one another.[30] They see in darkness, with the eyes of faith and love, beyond concepts, by connaturality; and their surrender sanctions and deepens the knowledge gained in their living encounter with the Triune God.

Can we go further beyond stating the fact of this "intuition" of the Trinity and suggesting the approach to this insight? The common Christian experience is fulfilled with this more than satisfying encounter with the Triune God, and does not try to analyze it or to ask a detailed account of it. Christians rest on the rock of their faith, and rightly so. They live by their faith, without reflexive analysis of its psychology. But we may mention in passing the striking confirmation of this experience found in the testimony of the mystics. No one can help being struck by the fact that so many of these privileged witnesses to the mysteries of grace build their spirituality, their theoretical and practical system of the life of grace, on a Trinitarian pattern.[31] Some more, some less, but nearly all of them in some measure, speak of the knowledge and love of the Father, Son and Holy Spirit, of the Triune God, and see in our sharing of the Trinitarian life the very structure of the life of grace. This testimony of the mystics confirms the psychology of our encounter with the Triune God.

We may conclude here this attempt at evaluating the meaning of the encounter with God. The analysis of the theology and psychology of what is the heart and center of the life of grace should help us to realize something of the depth of the mystery of grace. It should also have shown what hidden riches are brought to light in the personalistic approach to the mystery of grace, and above all it should be an invitation to an ever fuller living of our encounter with Christ and with the Triune God!

NOTES

1. Cf. P. De Haes, "Personalistische opvatting en voorstelling van de genadeleer," *Collectanea Mechliniensia*, 38 (1953), 301-330. See also J. Alfaro, S.J., "Persona y Gracia," in *Gregorianum*, 41 (1960), 5-29.

2. Cf. J. Mouroux, *Je crois en Toi. Structure personnelle de la foi* (Paris, 1948).

3. Cf. H. Schillebeeckx, O. P., *De Christusontmoeting als sacrament van de Godsontmoeting* (Antwerp, 1957); also "Sakramente als Organe der Gottesbegegnung" in *Fragen der Theologie Heute* (2nd ed., 1958), 379-401.

4. Cf. M. Nédoncelle, *La réciprocité des consciences* (Paris, 1942).

5. Cf. my article, "Sanctifying Grace and the Divine Indwelling" in *Theological Studies*, 14 (1953), 242-273.

6. *S. Th.* I, 43, 3.

7. Cf. above, n. 2.

8. Cf. St. Thomas, *In Boethium de Trinitate*, q. 3, a. 1, ad 4, "lumen fidei . . . est quasi sigillatio primae veritatis in mente."

9. Cf. above, n. 3.

10. For the present-day insistence on the *opus operantis* in the reception of the sacraments, cf. H. Schillebeeckx, *De sacramentele heilseconomie* (Antwerp, 1952); and L. Villette, *Foi et Sacrement 1* (Paris, 1959).

11. Cf. the Tridentine decree on justification. Ch. 7; Denzinger, *Enchiridion symbolorum*, 799.

12. Cf. my article, "Am I in the State of Grace?" in *Cross and Crown*, 11 (1959), 140-147.

13. Cf. "Trinitarian Indwelling according to Ruusbroec," *The Heythrop Journal*, 2 (1961).

14. Cf. J. Mouroux, *Expérience chrétienne* (Paris 1952); English *The Christian Experience* (London, 1955).

15. Cf. M. Nédoncelle, above, n. 4; also L. Jerphagnon, "Le corps et la communication des consciences," in *L'homme au regard de la foi* (Paris, 1959).

16. Cf. Jerphagnon, *art. cit.*

17. Cf. J. Mouroux, *Sens chrétien de l'homme* (Paris, 1945); English *The Meaning of Man*, (London, 1948); chs. 3 and 4.

18. Cf. *S. Th.* I, 29, 3 and 4.

19. Cf. F. Hofmann, "Glaubensgrundlagen der liturgischen Erneuerung" in *Fragen der Theologie Heute*, 485-515, the section "Der Christusglaube der Liturgie," 486-496.

20. Much of this paragraph is based on the unpublished course *Die Fide* of Fr. Ed. Dhanis, S.J.; also M. de la Taille, "Oraison contemplative" in *Recherches de science religieuse*, 9 (1919), 273-292; English *Contemplative Prayer* (London, 1926).

21. Cf. J. Mouroux, *Je crois en Toi*.

22. Compare St. Thomas, *S. Th.* II II, 29, ad 3, faith as *interior instinctus Dei invitantis*, and his teaching on the influence of the will in faith, *ibid. c.*

23. Cf. e.g., E. Mersch, *Théologie du Corps Mystique* (Paris, 1944), II, 173 ff. (supernatural order—relation to the Trinity); English

Theology of the Mystical Body, translated by C. Vollert (St. Louis, 1951), 461 ff.

24. Cf. for its description, e.g., Symbolum *Quicumque*, Denzinger, 39.

25. Cf. *S. Th.* I, 29.

26. Cf. *S. Th.* I, 30.

27. Cf. *S. Th.* I, 31.

28. Cf. Symbolum Toletanum, Denzinger, 19; or Symbolum Nicaeno-Constantinopolitanum, Denzinger, 86.

29. Compare the dark night of the soul in St. John of the Cross, with, on the part of the mystic, the setting aside of every conceptual representation.

30. As a matter of experience, the faithful believe the mystery of the Blessed Trinity, by a sort of connaturality given in the grace and light of faith, without normally experiencing any rational difficulty about the mystery.

31. As for example, Ruusbroec or St. Ignatius of Loyola.